REVOLUTIONARY LOVE

Creating a Culturally Inclusive Literacy Classroom

Kamania Wynter-Hoyte • Eliza Braden • Michele Myers
Sanjuana C. Rodriguez • Natasha Thornton

To teachers committed to equity.

Thank you for inspiring us to keep searching for ways
to share this work with others.

Acquisitions editor: Lois Bridges
Editorial director: Sarah Longhi
Editor at large: Tonya Leslie
Development editor: Raymond Coutu
Senior editor: Shelley Griffin
Production editor: Danny Miller
Creative director: Tannaz Fassihi
Interior designer: Maria Lilja

Photos ©: Cover, Back Cover, 24, 57, 93, 97, 105, 129, 157, 168: Shutterstock.com; 17: top left: Harris & Ewing/Library of Congress; top center: Library of Congress; top right: C.M. Bell (Firm: Washington, D.C.)/Library of Congress; center left: Center for Puerto Rican Studies, Library and Archives; bottom left: New York Public Library; bottom right: The University of Texas at San Antonio; 23: kali9/Getty Images; 35: New York Public Library; 63: Pictorial Press Ltd/Alamy Images; 71: FatCamera/Getty Images; 92: left: PictureLux/The Hollywood Archive/Alamy Images; top right: Photo by Robert Giard, Copyright Estate of Robert Giard; bottom left: Everett Collection Historical/Alamy Images; bottom right: IanDagnall Computing/Alamy Images; 123, Back Cover: STEEX/Getty Images; 161: FatCamera/Getty Images; All other icons: The Noun Project; All other photos, courtesy of the authors.

Additional credits ©: 17: Excerpt from "Love Is Revolutionary" © 1978 by Kalamu ya Salaam. Reprinted by permission of the author; 86: Excerpt from "Raised by Women" © 2003 by Kelly Norman Ellis. Reprinted by permission of the author; 91: Image from "The Nature of Emotions" by Robert Plutchik, 2001. Reprinted by permission of *American Scientist*, Magazine of Sigma Xi, The Scientific Research Honor Society.
All rights reserved.

CONTENTS

Acknowledgments 8

Foreword by Gloria Swindler Boutte 10

Introduction: What Does It Mean to Be a Teacher
Who Embraces Revolutionary Love? 12

Chapter 1 **REVOLUTIONARY LOVE IN ACTION** 18

Principles of Teachers Who Embrace Revolutionary Love 19

**PART I: KNOW YOURSELF, YOUR SYSTEMS,
AND YOUR PRACTICES** 23

Chapter 2 **KNOW YOURSELF** 24

Understanding Culture and Identity 25

    Self-Examination Activity 1: Identity Web: Who Am I? 25

    Self-Examination Activity 2: Labeling Dimensions
    of My Social Identity 28

    Self-Examination Activity 3: Social Identity and Stereotypes:
    But That's Not Me 30

Critical Self-Examination: Biases Are Real 32

In Summary 34

Chapter 3 *KNOW YOUR SYSTEMS* 35

A Historical Timeline 36

Teaching Is Political 38

    Self-Examination Activity: Investigating Practices and Policies for Bias 41

The Normalization of Whiteness 44

    Policy and Language/Positioning of Students 44

In Summary 49

Chapter 4 *KNOW YOUR LITERACY INSTRUCTION AND CURRICULUM* 50

What Is Literacy? 51

Children's Literature as Windows, Mirrors, Sliding Glass Doors 52

Literacy as Historically Political 53

    Teaching Hard History 53

    Literacy Today... Still Political 56

    Self-Examination Activity: Creating Your Literacy Timeline 57

Examining Curricula 60

    Curriculum Audit: Questions to Consider 62

    Guidelines for Selecting Children's Literature 64

Examining Classroom Libraries 65

    Classroom Library Audit: Questions to Consider 65

    Class Activity: Classroom Library Audit With Students 67

In Summary 70

PART II: ENGAGE WITH STUDENTS, FAMILIES, AND COMMUNITIES 71

Chapter 5 **ENGAGE WITH STUDENTS** 72

Embracing Culturally Inclusive Norms in the Classroom 73

    Class Activity: Co-Creating Classroom Norms With Students 77

Children's Books That Build Community 81

Community-Building Activities That Honor Students' Identities 83

    Where I'm From Poems 83

    "Raised By" Poems 86

    Honey, I Love Poems 88

    Oral History Activities 89

Building Authenticity in a Classroom Community 90

    Morning Meeting/Family Time 90

    Mindfulness 91

In Summary 92

Chapter 6 **ENGAGE WITH FAMILIES AND COMMUNITIES** 93

Microaggressions Toward Families 95

    Self-Examination Activity: Mining Your Microaggressions 95

    Common Microaggressions Experienced by Black and Latine Families 96

Broadening Our Conceptions of Home and Families 97

    Committing to Unlearning and Relearning 97

Culturally Inclusive Practices With Families 99

    Name Stories 101

    Intergenerational Writing 102

    Where I'm From Memoirs 103

    Family Photo Stories 103

    Family Read-Alouds 103

    Family Book Clubs 104

    Class and Family Text Sets 104

In Summary 104

PART III: PRACTICE LIBERATING LITERACY INSTRUCTION 105

Chapter 7 LIBERATE LANGUAGES 106

Honoring Home Languages 106

    Self-Examination Activity 1: Exploring Your Beliefs About Language 108

Translanguaging: A Humanizing and Transformative Approach 111

    What Is Translanguaging? 111

African American Language (AAL) 113

    AAL: A Historical Perspective 114

    Self-Examination Activity 1: Unpacking AAL 116

    Culturally Inclusive Unit Plans 116

Mexican American Language (MxAL) 124

    MxAL: A Historical Perspective 124

    Self-Examination Activity 2: Rebutting Microaggressions About Language 127

    Culturally Inclusive Unit Plans 127

In Summary 128

Chapter 8 LIBERATE READER'S WORKSHOP 129

An Overview of Reader's Workshop 131

    Getting to Know Students as Readers 131

    Interactive Read-Aloud 134

    Mini-Lessons 141

    Independent Reading 145

Reading Assessment Through a Revolutionary Love Lens 146

    Kidwatching and Notetaking 147

    The Oral Reading Record 151

Small-Group Instruction Through a Revolutionary Love Lens 151

    Teaching Reading Based on Needs 152

    Creating Book Clubs 153

In Summary 156

Chapter 9 **LIBERATE WRITER'S WORKSHOP** 157

An Overview of Writer's Workshop 158

Common Writing Practices 159

Self-Examination Activity 1: Reflecting on Writing Practices 161

Getting to Know Students as Writers 161

Self-Examination Activity 2: Examining Your Beliefs
About Writing and Writers 163

Creating a Community of Writers 163

Mini-Lessons 167

Mentor Texts 170

Conferring: Providing Feedback Through a Revolutionary Love Lens 176

Sharing Work Through a Revolutionary Love Lens 177

Writing Assessment Through a Revolutionary Love Lens 178

Self-Examination Activity 3: Noticing Strengths 179

Holistic Rubrics 179

Writing Celebrations 182

In Summary 186

Closing Reflection 185

Children's Books Cited 186

References 188

Index 190

ACKNOWLEDGMENTS

We want to acknowledge those who have paved the way for us to write this book about revolutionary love. Educators and scholars who have placed love at the center of their work. Educators who taught for liberation because they knew education was freedom. Scholars who write about the best of Black and Latine children. We could not write about revolutionary love without the culturally informed and liberatory pedagogies that you affirm, practice, and share with us through your work.

Thank you to our stellar Scholastic editorial team: Tonya Leslie, Sarah Longhi, Raymond Coutu, Shelley Griffin, Danny Miller, Tannaz Fassihi, and Maria Lilja. Your suggestions ensured that we were clear in the important message that we wanted to convey to teachers. Thank you for your collaborative effort to help us see our vision become a reality with this book.

Many thanks to Lois Bridges for believing in the possibilities of sharing revolutionary love with teachers.

We would like to thank the teachers who have opened their classrooms to us over the years to give us insights around the reciprocity of revolutionary love between teachers and students. Special recognition goes to the teachers whose brilliant practices we highlight in this book: Mukarramah Smith, Terri Washington, Valente' Gibson, Caitlyn McDonald, Jacqui Witherspoon, and Sara Suber. We are thankful for your willingness to open your classrooms to us and for allowing us to share the joy they bring to children. We are indebted to your commitment to loving your students enough to (re)envision curriculum in loving ways.

We also want to thank the countless students that we have worked with. We all began our careers as classroom teachers. Thank you for allowing us to learn from you and with you. You continue to influence the work that we do today and every day for our own children and the children that sit in schools today.

To our mentors, we want to express our deepest gratitude for contributing to our growth as teachers and scholars. Thank you to Amy Seely Flint, Susi Long, Gloria Boutte, Akosua Lessenne, Tasha Laman, Meir Muller, and the countless others who epitomize revolutionary love.

We want to end by thanking our families. We express our gratitude to our parents:

- Carmen and Leon Wynter (Kamania)
- Connie and Leroy Kennedy and James and Judy Mincey (Eliza)
- Elijah and Sandra Gillens (Michele)
- Eulalia and Baltazar Carrillo (Sanjuana)
- Tony and Vickie Adams (Natasha)

Thank you to our loving partners who have supported us unconditionally as we pursue the work our souls must have. We love you, Tye (Kamania), Cedric (Eliza), Luis (Sanjuana), and Eric (Natasha). We are inspired by our own children—Langston, Nyla, Dominic, Kailon, Donnovan, Olivia, Summer, Zoya, Samuel, Camila, EJ, and Cam—to continue to seek ways to help teachers embody revolutionary love.

FOREWORD

by Gloria Swindler Boutte

Teachers are amazing. And don't let anyone convince you otherwise. At a moment in time when teachers are being vilified for so many reasons, from so many angles, this book provides a healthy dose of love to buffer and heal. You will feel embraced and energized after reading it.

"What's love got to do with it?" you may ask. Everything. The authors explain what revolutionary loving teachers believe, know, and do. For example, those teachers see and honor the humanity, intelligence, and ethnic and racial identities of their students, as well as their linguistic practices, and use their knowledge to build curriculum for and with their students. Revolutionary love helps all students by disrupting messages of racial inferiority, omission, and inaccurate historical representations. I wish that my children and grandchildren had been assigned revolutionary loving teachers—teachers who would have honored their whole selves.

For that matter, I wish I had been assigned those teachers! My K–12 literacy timeline was filled with books and stories that did not reflect my family and community, thus sending a message that I was not part of the norm and not worthy of respect. Thankfully, my community offered ongoing, positive messages about Black people, our culture, our literacies, and our histories. We learned it through old black-and-white films about Black heroes and heroines such as Harriet Tubman and Frederick Douglass. We learned it through the music and dances in our homes and communities. But it would have been nice to also have our culture, literacies, and histories honored in school. As Toni Morrison said in *Beloved*, "Love is or love ain't. Thin love ain't love at all." The "love" of Black people that we received in school was thin indeed. Revolutionary love is thick, informed, and transformational.

Through lessons, strategies, text sets, and much more, the authors—five Black and Brown educators—make it clear that revolutionary loving teachers *know* themselves as well as students, families, and communities. To that end, they offer numerous self-examination activities for readers to engage in the process of transforming traditional literacy spaces into revolutionary ones, particularly for Black and Brown students who are often made invisible or hyper-visible in schools. They share their wisdom and firsthand classroom experiences—decades of insight based on culturally informed research.

Revolutionary Love will help you regain that joy by showing what is possible through examples of teachers and students in vibrant, revolutionary classrooms.

Revolutionary loving teachers welcome and build on *any* languages that children speak. By doing so, they help students maintain linguistic and cultural bonds with their families and communities. But make no mistake, revolutionary love, as the name implies, requires fundamental changes in curriculum, instruction, assessment, family-school relations, and so many other critical aspects of teaching and learning. *What does revolutionary love look like in classrooms?* Ideally, it permeates the teaching of literacy curriculum standards. It shapes and guides the implementation of policies in intentional and systemic ways. Not only is the curriculum and instruction liberated, but so are the students, teachers, and families.

Ask yourself: How refreshing and energizing would it be to regain the joy of teaching that you had when you entered the profession? *Revolutionary Love* will help you regain that joy by showing what is possible through examples of teachers and students in vibrant, revolutionary classrooms. You will see how excellent teachers of literacy impact not only their students, but also their families and communities. By following the advice that is engagingly offered, you will not only build your students' reading, writing, speaking, and listening skills, but also their racial literacy. I predict you will enthusiastically read this book and return to it again and again as a resource. It will help you recall why you chose to teach in the first place—to be a purveyor of good and a creator of legacies of love among the children you teach and in the world.

Gloria Swindler Boutte
Associate Dean of Diversity, Equity, and Inclusion,
University of South Carolina
Carolina Distinguished Professor, Early Childhood Education

WHAT DOES IT MEAN TO BE A TEACHER WHO EMBRACES REVOLUTIONARY LOVE?

Our beloved ancestor Maya Angelou presented us with a challenge that guided us throughout the creation of this book: "Do the best you can until you know better. Then when you know better, do better." We wrote *Revolutionary Love* to help all of us do better by the children we teach. Most of us reading this book, authors included, were educated in a Eurocentric system that was not inclusive or affirming of diverse races, languages, and cultures. As we matriculated through our education, our experiences with schooling shaped our beliefs about the nature of teaching, teachers, and students, and is largely responsible for how we constructed our initial teacher identities. Our teacher prep programs were extensions of our PreK–12 experiences, giving little voice to Black and Latine scholars to show us the way when teaching children, in their genius and beauty. As such, when we entered teaching, we replicated many of the practices we experienced as students.

> "Do the best you can until you know better. Then when you know better, do better."
>
> —MAYA ANGELOU

We're sure that, at some moment in your career, you've professed your love for the children you work with. Most teachers have. Statements such as, "I fell in love with teaching," "I love working with children," or "I love all children," are common; and who would refute such positive, caring statements? If we were to ask if you love the children you work with, you are more than likely to respond with a resounding, "Yes, of course." And based on this lens, such a response would be accurate. But then the question becomes, *What does that love look like?* Do your practices honor the children's culture? Are there classroom artifacts that tell you where the students come from? Do you know and honor the languages your students speak, and the essence of who they are?

We draw on the term *revolutionary love*, first coined by Kalamu ya Salaam (1978), as we conceptualize our vision. Love transcends caring about children. Love is action-packed. How we behave as educators is an expression of that love. Maya Angelou's opening quote speaks to the importance of our actions as demonstrations of the capacity of the love and care that we show our students. When we think about *how much we care*, we think about love and care that are steeped in our commitment to improve our collective humanity. We think about love and care that is bold, and we are willing to do more than care *about* the children we teach, but to care *for* them in ways that require action to change practices that marginalize them.

> "Love is as love does, and it is our responsibility to give children love. When we love children, we acknowledge by every action that... they have rights—that we respect and uphold their rights. Without justice there can be no love."
>
> **—bell hooks**

Scholars such as Paulo Freire (1972) have considered the act of love and the art of teaching. He wrote that "love is an act of courage, not of fear, love is commitment to other(s)." What does courageous love look like in a classroom? What does fearless love look like? What does love look like to committed educators? How do we love children beyond the surface level? How do we love students' histories beyond Black History Month and National Hispanic Heritage Month? How do our daily practices intentionally honor Black and Latine children, and their communities and languages?

Revolutionary teachers Kaitlin Jones and Mukarramah Smith with their first-grade students.

INTRODUCTION: WHAT DOES IT MEAN TO BE A TEACHER WHO EMBRACES REVOLUTIONARY LOVE?

13

Revolutionary love helps all students by disrupting messages of racial inferiority, omission, and inaccurate historical representations. Teachers who embrace revolutionary love understand the tremendous responsibility of shaping the next generation of lawmakers, medical professionals, financial managers, and teachers who will either perpetuate racism or disrupt it. Teachers who embrace revolutionary love understand that this disruption is twofold. First, it involves cultivating spaces for Black and Latine children that affirm their brilliance in an educational system and curriculum that has failed them. Second, it involves cultivating spaces so that non-Black and non-Latine children recognize the brilliance of their peers' communities, histories, and heritages. While we focus on teaching with and about Black and Latine communities, it does not mean we are neglecting other groups. We stand firm that we cannot be anti-racist if we are homophobic, transphobic, anti-immigrant, anti-Muslim, and so forth (Kendi, 2019). We focus primarily on Black and Latine children because anti-Black racism is the most dominant form of racism in the United States (Dumas & Ross, 2016) and Latines account for over half of the country's population growth. This does not mean we are ignoring other forms of diversity, because Black and Latine populations are not monolithic. One can study Black and Latine children while exploring ethnicity, language, gender, religion, immigration, abilities, and many other forms of identity.

Why "Latine"?

We have chosen to use the term *Latine* in this book to describe individuals who identify as Latino/a/x. In the interest of using a broadly accepted gender-neutral term, we looked at a frequently cited study undertaken by the Pew Research Center, which found only one in four Latinos are aware of the term *Latinx*, and just three percent say they use it to describe themselves (Noe-Bustamante, Mora, & Lopez, 2020). We have adopted *Latine* as a more linguistically accessible, but imperfect alternative. We recognize that some readers may self-identify using other terms.

Our Journeys

Our journeys toward becoming teachers who embrace revolutionary love has led us to these understandings. This book highlights our revolutionary love stories: the stories of five Black and Latine women authors who embrace multiple identities: African American, Mexican American, cisgender, immigrant, child of immigrant parents, heterosexual, able-bodied, middle class, and the list goes on. We each weave our stories throughout this book to connect our personal and professional experiences as we share our journeys toward revolutionary love as educators working alongside Black and Latine children and their families.

KAMANIA

Kamania's mission is inspired by her children Langston and Nyla. She hopes their teachers will honor and value their home languages, culture, and histories. They are the reason she does this work because countering anti-Blackness is important for all children; not just hers.

ELIZA

Eliza's advocacy for her Black and Latine students is rooted in the Black historical narratives that she learned from the Black women and community activists as a child in Savannah, Georgia. She understands that much of what she learned about her people came from Black spaces, like the Black church, salons, and Gullah/Geechie culture and traditions, and not her K–12 schooling. She used this knowledge to teach her Black and Latine elementary students that their culture is brilliant, sufficient, and beautiful.

MICHELE

Michele shares her journey through the continuous process of self-introspection that shifted the work she does with preservice teachers. Michele often quotes John Maxwell, who espouses, "A child doesn't care how much you know until he knows how much you care." The kind of care and revolutionary love that matter is rooted in liberation—liberation of oneself and others.

SANJUANA

Sanjuana's story stems from her identity as a Mexican teacher working with Latine students. Her experience as an immigrant learning to navigate a new culture and language shapes her work with students and teachers.

NATASHA

Natasha's journey involved unlearning Eurocentric teaching norms from years of navigating majority White educational spaces. She loved her students but was taught standards and a curriculum that wasn't so loving toward them. When she began studying the richness of Black language, culture, and history, she strengthened her racial identity and supported her students by having them do the same.

We wrote this book in honor of the Black and Latine teachers who have shown us how to teach with revolutionary love. We stand on their shoulders and build on their legacies, which are rooted in historical periods, movements, and events such as the Jim Crow Era, the Mexican Revolution, the Civil Rights Movement, the Black Lives Matter movement, and the bilingual education movement.

As Black and Latine teacher educators and former classroom teachers and administrators, we have witnessed the absence of revolutionary love from the classroom. We have also witnessed teachers who profess love but fail to understand that an uninformed love for Black and Latine children is not love at all. And whether teachers intend to or not, they are harming their students. We also know well what love looks, sounds, and feels like for Black and Latine children. This book is a journey to uncover such love. We start with Salaam (1978), who teaches us to love our students in ways that matter.

we are lovers
and revolutionaries
conscious that our
commitment to each other
serves higher purpose
than limited personal pleasure
—KALAMU YA SALAAM

We draw from the courage, compassion, commitment, and foresight of teachers who are often not mentioned or studied in teacher education preparatory programs, such as Fanny Jackson Coppin, Jovita Idár, Anna J. Cooper, Pura Belpré, Mary McLeod Bethune, Antonia Pantoja, Jaime Escalante, and many, many others.

(Clockwise from top left) Mary McLeod Bethune, Fanny Jackson Coppin, Anna J. Cooper, Jovita Idár, Pura Belpré, Antonia Pantoja

Chapter 1

REVOLUTIONARY LOVE IN ACTION

Revolutionary love isn't just a theory—it's an action. Loving our students in a revolutionary way means recognizing systems that are inherently racist and fighting against them. As teachers, we must understand that there are policies, laws, and practices that place Black and Latine children at a disadvantage and we must work to disrupt and replace them. We draw on the scholars of color who laid a foundation for our work: Gloria Boutte, Lisa Delpit, Geneva Gay, Jacqueline Jordan Irvine, Gloria Ladson-Billings, Luis Moll, Angela Valenzuela, and so many others who have studied aspects of education related to revolutionary love.

Educators cultivate revolutionary love when they see and honor the humanity, intelligence, ethnic and racial identities, and linguistic practices of their students and use them to build curriculum for and with their students. They are not afraid to see color. They are not restricted by state mandates and prescribed curriculum. They understand that anti-racist, decolonized, and culturally relevant teaching is important for all children because our curriculum is filled with inaccurate, incomplete, and distorted information about people of color that casts them in a negative light and supports Whiteness as the norm (Derman-Sparks & Ramsey, 2006).

Our ancestor bell hooks said, "Until we live in a culture that not only respects but also upholds basic civil rights for children, most children will not know love" (1999, p. 51). Therefore, we find it morally, ethically, and intellectually necessary to affirm the humanity of Black and Latine children through culturally relevant and inclusive teaching.

To affirm the humanity of our students, to love them, we must first *see* them. A colorblind approach is not equitable practice. In fact, a colorblind approach is the antithesis of revolutionary love because when educators are colorblind, they do not see the histories of brilliance as well as oppression and resistance of students of color. If educators do not see their students, they will not be able to recognize issues of racism they face in and out of school, and therefore, will not be able to advocate for and with them. If educators do not see their students, they cannot truly love them.

Principles of Teachers Who Embrace Revolutionary Love

Our principles of revolutionary love are influenced by the traditions of Black and Latine teachers whose work is, and has always been, loving and liberatory (Anzaldúa, 1987; King & Swartz, 2018; Valenzuela, 1999). Based on that research and teaching, we use the following framework to organize our book.

Believe	Know	Do
Teachers who embrace revolutionary love understand that what they believe is foundational to the ways they engage with students.	**Teachers who embrace revolutionary love understand the importance of knowing their students, their pedagogy, and the resources they use to teach their students.**	**Teachers who embrace revolutionary love understand that what they do—their practice--needs to be loving, liberatory, and affirming, and center their students' identities and cultural heritages.**
They are committed to examining and disrupting any beliefs that are deficit-oriented so that their practices are affirming of the students they teach.	They are knowledgeable about their students' cultural and linguistic identities and the systems that marginalize their students, as well as the practices that affirm the students they teach.	They intentionally create learning communities for and with students so that students can learn at their full potential and feel seen, heard, and valued.

TEACHERS WHO EMBRACE REVOLUTIONARY LOVE BELIEVE IN:

- recognizing the innate brilliance, potential, and cultural richness of their Black and Latine students.
- honoring the uniqueness of their students.
- celebrating the interconnectedness of our shared humanity, recognizing that *I am because we are.*
- taking action for liberation and justice.
- disrupting "White supremacist norms" (Johnson, Bryan, & Boutte, 2019).
- moving beyond the surface-level statements (e.g., "I love all my students the same and don't see color").
- changing the world one person at a time.

TEACHERS WHO EMBRACE REVOLUTIONARY LOVE KNOW:

- themselves, and interrogate their systems and practices. Before we address instruction and inclusive teaching, we embark on a micro and macro examination of self and systems at large. We include exercises that will provide a space for you to investigate your multiple identities, cultures, and experiences, and how you bring them into the classroom. In addition, we will explore how social, political, and historical contexts shape your classroom every single day (Chapters 1 and 2).
- their students, families, and (other) communities. We unpack how teachers, leaders, students, and families are interconnected and why this work is important for the school, and for humanity.
- that everyone in the classroom community holds knowledge (not just the teacher). Valuing the knowledge of our students and communities offers opportunities to dismantle oppressive systems and co-create opportunities for changing practice to center students and their families (Chapters 4 and 5).

TEACHERS WHO EMBRACE REVOLUTIONARY LOVE DO:

- center the experiences, histories, languages, and richness of Black and Latine communities in the curriculum. For too long, Black and Latine histories and experiences have been erased from classroom curriculum. Centering this knowledge benefits everyone (Chapters 6 and 8).

- liberate their literacy instruction. The Reverend Dr. Martin Luther King, Jr. said, "No one is free until we are all free." Teachers who practice revolutionary love are committed to loving Black and Latine children. They are convinced that opening new worlds for all students will serve in the best interest of humanity. They are committed to centering the literacies of Black and Latine children by valuing their existence in classrooms. When teachers honor students' stories, experiences, languages, and digital literacy and associated platforms such as TikTok, they teach from a liberating stance that fights against a Eurocentric curriculum that fails to center the lives of Black and Latine students.

The book is designed to support you on your journey to revolutionary love.

Part I provides opportunities for self-reflection and the investigation of our own belief systems.

Part II provides opportunities to foster interconnectedness in your classroom and beyond.

Part III demonstrates how the principles of revolutionary love unfold in elementary school classrooms. We share stories of our own journeys along the way.

Recently, there has been a national surge of legislators proposing laws to prohibit teachers from teaching issues of race and racism, purporting, by many, that they make White students feel bad for being White. It is critical for all of us to understand that making one feel bad, whether a student or teacher, is not the purpose of anti-racist teaching. Freire reminds us that "love is at the foundation of dialogue" and if you enter this space with overwhelming feelings of guilt, you will miss the opportunity "and commitment, because love is dialogical, an act of bravery, love cannot be sentimental, but is an act of freedom, it must not serve as a pretext for manipulation" (1970, p. 78).

Teachers who embrace revolutionary love know that to be a democratic country, all members must be free from oppression. They do not only teach the racial injustices of this country, but also the long history of White people who fought for equity because of concerns for humanity. Those people include Jeremiah Rankin, an abolitionist of slavery; Helen Hunt Jackson, a poet who fought against the mistreatment of Indigenous Americans; Rabbi Abraham Joshua Heschel, a Polish-born American Jewish theologian who actively participated in the Civil Rights Movement and marched alongside Dr. Martin Luther King, Jr. and Senator John Lewis in Selma, Alabama; Joan Trumpauer Mulholland, an American civil rights activist, Freedom Rider, and member of Student Nonviolent Coordinating Committee (SNCC); and most recently James Tyson, who used his White privilege to protect Bree Newsome as she climbed a pole to remove the confederate flag at the state capitol in South Carolina.

This book is for educators, teacher educators, and school administrators who seek to cultivate the power of revolutionary love. As you read it and engage in its activities, be prepared to question, stretch, and challenge yourself to love more deeply than you thought you could.

Throughout the book, we include many classroom examples, photos, and student artifacts to illustrate how revolutionary love fosters an anti-racist classroom. However, this is not a one-size-fits-all approach; this work should look different across spaces. As you embark on this journey of self-reflection and action, we hope you remember the words of our ancestor Dr. Asa Hilliard, a professor of urban education whose expertise included ancient Africa, history, culture, and curriculum: "I have never encountered any children in any group who are not geniuses. There is no mystery on how to teach them. The first thing you do is treat them like human beings, and the second thing you do is love them." This book is for educators, teacher educators, and school administrators who seek to cultivate the power of revolutionary love. As you read it and engage in its activities, be prepared to question, stretch, and challenge yourself to love more deeply than you thought you could.

Part I

KNOW YOURSELF, YOUR SYSTEMS, AND YOUR PRACTICES

Chapter 2

KNOW YOURSELF

Teachers who embrace revolutionary love believe that before we can honor the humanity, intelligence, racial identities, and linguistic practices of our students, we must examine ourselves. We must investigate the ideologies we bring into our classrooms and schools, and explore our cultures and identities in terms of race, ethnicity, gender, class, language, sexual orientation, religion, ability, age, and so forth. Why? Because culture and identity inform who we are, how we make decisions, how we experience the world, and how we view, engage, and interact with others. In short, our identities impact everything, whether we are conscious of it or not.

This chapter is designed to assist you on your lifelong journey of practicing revolutionary love. Its self-examination activities will help you reflect on yourself, your practices, and the systems in which you live and work. We hope they will awaken your consciousness and allow you to see the world in a different way, knowing that we are all interconnected. So, let the journey begin.

Understanding Culture and Identity

Each of us has myriad social identities that influence our experiences in life and our interactions with others—identities that are steeped in the culture in which we were socialized. As teachers, we do not leave our identities in the school parking lot before entering the building. We bring them into our classrooms, and they influence the decisions we make. The goal of the three activities that follow is to highlight the multiple dimensions of your identity. The first one is designed to help you begin to answer the question, Who am I? So, grab your favorite pen and notebook, and let's get started.

SELF-EXAMINATION ACTIVITY 1
IDENTITY WEB: WHO AM I?

Take a moment to think about who you are as a cultural and social being. To gain the most from this activity, be open to it, take the necessary time to complete it, be honest, and intentionally and thoughtfully reflect on what you learn.

Steps

1. On a blank page in your notebook, draw a circle in the center and write your name inside it.

2. In surrounding smaller circles, list dimensions of your identity that you consider to be the most important in defining you. Include as many as possible. (See example below.)

3. Add illustrations if you like.

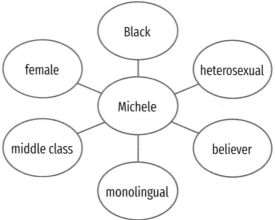

Now, look over your list. Pick one identity. What does this mean to you? In what ways do you operate in this identity? When are you most aware of it? When are you least aware of it?

As you can see, the dimensions of your identity make you who you are. They are woven into the fabric of your family, your ancestors, and children you may have and/or those to come. Your identity is influenced by your friends and foes, your community and neighbors, and your intimate relationships and heartbreaks. It is also influenced by the messages you receive through social media, the news, radio broadcasts, etc. It determines what you eat, wear, and dream. In short, your identity is largely determined by the people, places, and time in which you live. You are continuously socialized into the systems that govern it. We are all cultural beings. We have social identities (race, class, ethnicity, gender, age, religious beliefs, natural language, sexual orientation, ability, family structure, and nationality) that are framed by the society we live in.

Your identity is largely determined by the people, places, and time in which you live. You are continuously socialized into the systems that govern it. We are all cultural beings.

Some dimensions of your social identities offer you agency, privilege, and/or benefits because they closely align with the dominant group or the group that holds power. Consequently, other dimensions of your social identity deny you agency, privilege, and/or benefits. They may marginalize you or relegate you to unimportant or powerless positions, as determined by the dominant group. Let's look at two examples from Michele.

UNPACKING DIMENSIONS OF MICHELE'S IDENTITY

I am a speaker of English. In the society that I live (USA), that affords me privileges. For example, all the correspondences I receive in my language are accessible for me. I can easily move through life because my language is the language used by the dominant group. I usually do not think about this dimension of my identity a lot. But I do think about it when I am in the company of those whose first language is not English. For example, when I was an elementary school principal, I had a large student population of Spanish speakers. I remember the frustration and vulnerability I experienced when trying to maintain lines of communication with them and their families. I resorted to relying on one of my fourth-grade students, James, to translate important messages in Spanish for me. There was always that nagging uncertainty about his translations—about their level of accuracy. But as an English-only speaker with limited professional translation services, I had to use what was available, and I was grateful to James.

Another dimension of my identity is my race. I am Black. In a society that privileges Whiteness, being Black does not afford me agency. Here is an example of just that. A few years ago, a White colleague and I decided to co-teach a course in culturally relevant pedagogy for two groups of predominantly White, female preservice teachers. My colleague and I met each week to discuss the course content, grade students' work, and study their feedback for our research. At the end of the semester, my colleague earned very positive student evaluations. Some of her students applauded her for being brave enough to tackle issues of race as a White woman.

I, on the other hand, received less-than-glowing evaluations. Many of my students complained that all I did was talk about race. My colleague and I surmised that one reason for the differences in responses was that the students were more accepting of her delivery of the content because they, being White females like her, could more easily relate to her than to me, a Black female teaching the same content. Research (Drake, Auletto, & Cowen, 2019) suggests that Black professors routinely receive poor evaluations compared to their White colleagues, even when teaching the same material.

Based on these examples, you can tell there are dimensions of my social identity that give me agency and others that marginalize me. I usually don't think about the social identities that give me agency. They typically go unnoticed. However, the dimensions that marginalize me are always at the forefront of my mind.

Now it is time for you to think about the dimensions of your social identity by labeling those dimensions and determining which ones offer you privileges and which ones don't.

LABELING DIMENSIONS OF MY SOCIAL IDENTITY

The goal of this activity is to delve deeper into dimensions of your social identity (race, class, ethnicity, gender, age, religious beliefs, natural language, sexual orientation, ability, family structure, nationality, etc.) and to identify the messages you receive from the dominant culture, or the group that holds power.

Steps

1. Revisit the list you created in the first activity.
2. Look across it and categorize the dimensions of your identity based on the following: race, class, ethnicity, gender, age, religious beliefs, natural language, sexual orientation, ability, family structure, and nationality.
3. Put a plus sign beside those dimensions for which society provides you agency and a minus sign beside those for which it doesn't, and you feel marginalized. (See example below.)
4. Choose one of the dimensions of your social identity and reflect on a time when you felt especially proud to be associated with it—or on the affirming messages you receive from society about it. Write down your thoughts.
5. Choose another dimension and reflect on a time when it was particularly painful to be associated with it—or on the negative messages you receive from society about it. Write down your thoughts.

My Social Identity	Identity Type	Agency (+) or Oppression (–)
Black	Race	–
Female	Gender	–
Monolingual English Speaker	Linguistic	+
Believer	Religion	+
Middle class	Social class	+
Heterosexual	Sexuality	+

When you reflect on a dimension of your social identity that makes you feel a sense of agency, it is likely because you frequently receive affirming messages about that dimension. When you reflect on a dimension that makes you feel oppressed, it is likely because you frequently receive negative, stereotypical messages about that dimension. We offer the following questions to consider as you continue this process.

6. Reflect on this activity by considering these questions:

   - How have the systems in which I have been socialized caused me to humanize, sympathize, and value White people while dehumanizing Black and Latine people? By systems we mean schools, workplaces, religious spaces, businesses, healthcare facilities, and a host of other spaces. For example, when you turn on the television, who do you see as the norm? What race do you see in most commercials? Who is tokenized? In terms of other identities, what structures of families are portrayed? What types of families are privileged and pitied? Who is described as the all-American family? Who is depicted as beautiful? Are traditional gender roles displayed?

   - When you were a child, whose identities were affirmed daily? Did most of your teachers and classmates look like you? Speak the same language as you? Did the books feature families, communities, and experiences that were familiar to you? Did the pictures on the walls of your school feature people that look like you? How were communities of color depicted? Did you mostly learn about Black and Latine history during designated months? Did your Black history lessons begin with slavery? In the month of November, did you dress up as an Indigenous person or pilgrim? Did the school calendar observe your religious holidays?

   - What are your childhood experiences with Black and Latine communities? Did your family patronize Black and Latine local businesses? Use Black and Latine healthcare providers? Did you attend celebrations that are different from your own (e.g., quinceañera, Black family cookouts, etc.)? Did you attend religious services different from your own? Did your childhood community embrace multilingualism?

To help you dig a little deeper, we want you to do one more activity. Yes, one more, please.

SOCIAL IDENTITY AND STEREOTYPES: BUT THAT'S NOT ME

The goal of this activity is to identify the messages you receive from the mainstream. We ask you to reflect on whether those messages are true and inclusive, or stereotypical, and the impact they have on you.

Steps

1. Choose a dimension of your social identity about which you receive negative messages.
2. Take about five minutes to write down stereotypical messages you have heard about that dimension.
3. Strike the stereotypes that don't accurately describe you.
4. Reflect on this activity by considering these questions:
   - What did you notice?
   - How did you feel when you wrote about the dimension of your identity that you were most proud of?
   - Do you capitalize on those dimensions of your identity that hold power?
   - Do you use your power to help others?
   - How do you feel about those dimensions of your identity that marginalize you in society?
   - From what stereotypes do you disassociate?
   - What can you do to challenge what others assume about you?
   - From where do we get stereotypical messages about others?
   - What harm may those stereotypical messages cause?
   - How can we eliminate stereotypes?
   - What implications does this have for you as a person in a diverse world?
   - What implications does this have for you as a teacher?

By engaging in these activities, we hope you see that you are far more than the sum of your parts.

Teachers who embrace revolutionary love understand that the dimensions of our social identity intersect to impact our whole being. Dr. Kimberlé Crenshaw (1989) coined the term *intersectionality* to describe how class, race, gender, and other dimensions of social identity overlap with one another. For example, Michele is not just a Black person. She is also a cisgender, heterosexual, middle-class, able-bodied female, and so much more.

> Teachers who embrace revolutionary love understand that the dimensions of our social identity intersect to impact our whole being.

Furthermore, the dimensions of identity not only intersect, but the messages we receive about them can shift across time and context. For example, as a Black, educated, middle-class, single mother of two daughters, Michele receives positive, affirming messages from her sorority sisters, who admire her strength and resiliency, which have contributed to her independence and accomplishments. However, members of her church group take a more sympathetic stance based on Michele beating the odds as a divorcée who is raising children on her own.

Still, it is important that we do not deflect from the focus on race because different social identities are impacted by it. For example, the maternal outcomes for Black and White women are drastically different. In fact, Black women are three times more likely to die in pregnancy and postpartum than White women (MacDorman et al., 2021). And a study from Rutgers New Jersey Medical School reveals that Black and Latine children are more likely than White children to experience undiagnosed autism (Wiggins, et al., 2019).

Michele and her daughters

Critical Self-Examination: Biases Are Real

Now that you have become more aware of your social identities and the factors that shape them, let's take an honest look at deep-seated beliefs and biases you may have about others whose cultural norms differ from your own. Just as others may be quick to make assumptions about you, you may be quick to make assumptions about others. We all have learned biases—biases that are often implicit and impact our relationships and engagements with the people around us, even our students.

Critical self-reflection requires you to open yourself up to being vulnerable, honest, and willing to own your "-isms" and "-phobias" (e.g., racism, classism, sexism, xenophobia, transphobia, and homophobia). It is an imperative step for any teacher who wants to embrace revolutionary love. Rather than beating yourself up for your biases, it's healthier to acknowledge them and then deal with them by accepting two facts:

1. We are human beings and, as such, have been socialized to develop preconceived notions of others.
2. We have been socialized continuously to believe in the superiority of Whiteness and inferiority of all other races.

To support you in this process, we ask you to be vulnerable and open—and, in return, we will be, too. Here are some statements we want you to consider:

- *"These parents don't care about education."*
- *"I wish these parents came to conferences like they come to Field Day."*
- *"How can she know so young that she is not a girl?"*
- *"I've got to show the kids love because a lot of them don't get it at home."*
- *"If they come to America, they should learn English."*
- *"How can I teach them to read when they don't have any literacy experiences?"*

We wish we could say that these statements came from other teachers, or that we never have or never would make such statements. But we can't. We have participated in discussions that centered on blaming and judging families, and pitying children. The next story highlights Natasha's experience as a teacher at an elementary school with a predominantly Black student and teacher population, in which she owned her "-ism."

A NEED FOR REVOLUTIONARY LOVE

NATASHA'S STORY

In the early 2000s, when I was a classroom teacher, I truly loved my students and built close relationships with their families, just like most of my colleagues. Yet, I held views which were steeped in deficit beliefs (classism, etc.) about people who shared the same racial background, but who differed in other ways, such as their use of African American Language (AAL) in professional settings or socioeconomic status. As a Black woman, I had internalized deficit beliefs about my own racial group.

I would have conversations with colleagues that questioned how parents would buy expensive shoes but not school supplies, or how parents would attend Field Day but not academic conferences. It did not occur to me that what parents experienced as students shaped how and why they showed up at their own children's schools. Nor did I consider how the lack of flexibility in most jobs the parents had did not afford them the opportunity to take off for school functions. I was conditioned by dominant deficit beliefs not to value our rich cultural resources and I blamed Black people for the effects of systemic oppression.

In 2007, I took some reading endorsement courses at a local college and read *The Dream-Keepers: Successful Teachers of African American Children* by Dr. Gloria Ladson-Billings and *Other People's Children: Cultural Conflict in the Classroom* by Dr. Lisa Delpit. Also, while in my doctoral program, I had the opportunity to take social foundations courses from Dr. Joyce E. King. From those scholars, I learned about the innate strength and genius of Black people, the beauty of African American Language, and the long-lasting impact that systemic racism has had on Black communities. The deficit beliefs I held about some of my students and their families began to shift, but not without taking a hard look at myself. Introspection is difficult. Even 15 years later, I feel uncomfortable writing this. But I do it as part of the ongoing self-work that is necessary to disrupt deficit notions, and in hopes of prompting others to do the same.

Now it's your turn. Look back at the statements on page 32 and reflect in your notebooks on times you have made similar statements. Like Natasha found, are there any shifts you must make? How do you feel about this? Write about it in your notebook. And go even further. Do you have colleagues who may benefit from engaging in this introspective work? Are there people you know who might benefit from engaging in a book discussion? Yes, you can do this work on your own, but it may have an even greater impact if you do it with others.

In Summary

Teachers who embrace revolutionary love are willing to identify and own their "-isms" and/or "-phobias." This is an important step in understanding how biases work at the individual level (micro) and system level (macro). Self-examination is crucial in understanding ourselves as cultural beings and unpacking our biases (Gay, 2018; Howard, 2010). It is a constant process with no end point. It is not a checklist of activities, professional development opportunities, or book clubs alone. Your perception of students is influenced by the social messages you receive from your immediate circle and society at large (Thornton, 2017). Hence, while you are learning about your students' identities, you must reflect on your own. That is why we infuse this book with self-examination activities. As you complete them, identify steps you will take to change.

> Self-examination is crucial in understanding ourselves as cultural beings and unpacking our biases ... It is a constant process with no end point.

Take a break whenever you are overwhelmed or triggered. But stay the course, because discomfort often is a sign of learning. Many children of color and their families experience trauma and discomfort in schools across the country every day. So we urge you, on their behalf, to stay the course. You are on the cusp of something new and revolutionary.

Chapter 3

KNOW YOUR SYSTEMS

Teachers who embrace revolutionary love view their students, families, and communities through an asset-based lens, allowing them to better understand systemic racism and how it is the root cause for many of the social, economic, health care, and educational challenges that students of color face today.

Three Sioux boys (Wounded Yellow Robe, Henry Standing Bear, and Chauncey Yellow Robe) before they entered the Indian Boarding School (left) and three years later (right).

From its inception, the purpose of schooling in America was to socialize children through religion (DuFresne, 2018). In the 1700s, most teaching centered around being obedient and reading the Bible, and it was provided only to White children. The first Indian Boarding Schools opened under the motto "Kill the Indian, save the man" with the intent to "civilize" American Indians through religion. Prior to the Civil War, Black children were forbidden to attend school and legally prohibited from learning to read and write. After the Civil War, Black and Latine children were segregated from White children, and attended schools in underfunded facilities and with fewer resources.

A Historical Timeline

Let's take a closer look at a historical timeline to unpack how Indigenous, Black, and Latine children have been and continue to be subjected to inferior treatment in schools and in society.

1819 The Civilization Fund Act of 1819 provided government funds to Protestant missionary educators to form boarding schools for Native American children. Indigenous children were taken from their families and their own successful educational systems, and endured what Bettina Love calls "cultural genocide" (2019); they were physically and verbally abused for speaking their native language, forced to trade their religious/spiritual practices for Christianity, and were required to cut their hair. They were compelled to assimilate to American customs, which cost them their language and day-to-day ways of being. Yet, assimilation practices to rid Native Americans of, or "kill," their culture, customs, and heritage were seen as beneficial and necessary.

1830s States across the country began establishing laws that prohibited free and enslaved Africans from learning to read and write.

1850s The Fugitive Slave Act allowed Whites to capture enslaved Africans who had fled their enslavers and return them, even if they were in a free state. From there, they were convicted. This act made the federal government responsible for finding, returning, and convicting African Americans.

1855 California began requiring English-only instruction in public schools at all grade levels.

1860s While African Americans were set free by the Emancipation Proclamation, they faced Black Codes during Reconstruction, which limited their freedom and forced them into cheap labor.

1870 Texas required English-only instruction in public schools at all grade levels, impacting a huge number of Spanish-speaking students.

1896 Plessy v. Ferguson enacted "separate but equal" education in public schools for Blacks and Whites.

1918 Texas made it a criminal offense to use any language but English in public schools.

1930 Del Rio Independent School District v. Salvatierra was the first case in which Texas courts reviewed the actions of local school districts regarding the education of children of Mexican descent and proved that Del Rio ISD segregated Mexican American children based on race. Other school districts in Texas were challenged for maintaining separate schools for children of Mexican descent, which violated the Fourteenth Amendment of the United States Constitution.

1947 Mendez v. Westminster ruled that forced segregation of Mexican American students into separate "Mexican schools" was unconstitutional. This case began the end of the "separate but equal" doctrine influencing cases such as Hernandez v. Texas and Brown v. Board of Education.

| 1954 | **(May 3)** Hernandez v. Texas was a major civil rights case involving the 14th Amendment that changed the way Mexican Americans were viewed in the eyes of the government. Mexican Americans were originally viewed as White but constantly discriminated against. |

| 1954 | **(May 17)** Brown v. Board of Education of Topeka ruled that racial segregation of children in public schools was unconstitutional. Integration efforts led to a mass firing of Black teachers and increased the racial discrimination experienced by Black students and teachers in schools. |

Consider: What might be the lasting (generational) impact of these laws? Write about it in your notebook.

The impact of these decisions had devastating and long-lasting effects. For example, it wasn't until 159 years after the establishment of the Indian Boarding Schools that the Indian Welfare Act of 1978 finally allowed Native American parents to refuse their children's placement in those schools. While it is currently illegal to separate children based on race in schools, research shows that schools are more racially segregated today than they were in the 1960s.

Educational policies impact everything from the standards that are taught, to the tests that are administered, to instructional practices that are implemented—and, to an enormous degree, they've all grown out of the history described above that perpetuates racism in schools.

Many of those policies, even those that claim to promote equity in education, are in fact harmful, and further marginalize Black and Latine children (Ntiri, 2009). For example, No Child Left Behind (NCLB) and Race to the Top (RTT) were designed to "level the playing field for students who are disadvantaged, including students in poverty, minorities, students receiving special education services, and those who speak and understand limited or no English" (No Child Left Behind, 2001).

Schools became more accountable through testing and academic progress measures. They implemented initiatives such as Response to Intervention (RTI), Positive Behavior Interventions and Supports (PBIS), and English-only curricula—initiatives that claim to be "evidence-based," which means insight from parent and community members

Addressing Processes and Programs That Marginalize Black and Latine Students

Think about the types of data being collected to measure student success at your school. Then ask yourself what types are not being collected to highlight what students know. Whose norms, values, and knowledge are privileged? For example, are students being asked to ignore dimensions of their identity (language, cultural norms, etc.)? Are they being asked to conform to mainstream practices to maneuver in the program successfully? If so, re-center your approach and focus on students' assets. What linguistic resources are being underutilized? How can you and your colleagues build on those resources to strengthen literacy skills?

are often afterthoughts when developing such programs (Council, 2021), resulting in programs that are not culturally informed. They are threaded into the daily life of school, largely in the name of improving education for Black and Latine students, but they are deficit-based and, as Gloria Ladson-Billings claims, "designed to maintain a White supremacist master script" (1998) because they are often anchored in White-focused texts and encourage linguistic practices based on White middle-class discourse. And, in the process, Black and Latine children are disproportionately referred to special education programs over gifted and talented programs (Grissom & Redding, 2016). Additional examples of programs and policies like these are explained in Chapters 4–9.

Teaching Is Political

When most people hear the word *racism*, they think of overt examples such as the Ku Klux Klan, the Emanuel Nine, and the "Unite the Right" rally in Charlottesville, Virginia. However, racism is a smog we breathe in every day and do not even realize it (Tatum, 2017). It is embedded in laws and policies that have negatively impacted people of color for centuries. Racist historical and contemporary policies and their impact on people of color are outlined in the chart below. As you read, consider their long-term impact.

Policy	How It Marginalized People of Color
Naturalization Act of 1790	Automatically denied citizenship to people of color.
Indian Removal Act of 1830	Legalized the brutal removal of Indigenous people from east of the Mississippi River to the west.
Chinese Exclusion Act of 1882	Prohibited all immigration of Chinese laborers.
Anti-Drug Abuse Act of 1986	Set tougher laws for Black and Latine communities. For example, distribution of just five grams of crack cocaine carried a minimum five-year federal prison sentence, whereas for powder cocaine (primarily used by Whites) distribution of 500 grams (100 times more) carried the same sentence (aclu.org).
State Voter ID Requirement Laws (current)	Has significantly lowered the number of Black and Latine voters: approximately 1 in 10 Americans do not have government-issued photo IDs versus approximately 1 in 4 African Americans do not have government-issued photo IDs (aclu.org)

Racism impacts everyone. Ibram X. Kendi, bestselling author of *Stamped from the Beginning*, asserts, "Racist policy is any measure that produces or sustains racial inequity between racial groups." By policy, he means written and unwritten laws, rules, procedures, and processes that govern people. Kendi continues by stating, "There is no such thing as a nonracist or race-neutral policy. Every policy in every institution in every community in every nation is producing or sustaining either racial inequity or equity between racial groups" (2019).

So, if we are going to fully unpack racist policies, we must not only explore the people who are marginalized by them, but also the people who benefit from them. As you read each policy below, consider who benefits. What is the impact on those who don't benefit? What benefits are lost? What might be the long-term impact, both for people who benefit from the policy, and those who don't?

Policy	Who Benefits From It?
Naturalization Act of 1790	Only free White persons could become citizens of the United States. Native Americans and free and enslaved African Americans were excluded from this act.
Homestead Act of 1862	President Lincoln granted 246 million acres of western land (California and Texas) to "anyone," primarily White Americans, who could pay $1.25 to file an application, cultivate the land for five years, and file for the deed of ownership.
GI Bill of 1944	Aimed to help American WWII veterans adjust to civilian life by providing low-cost mortgages, low-interest loans, and financial support to majority White Americans. Most African American veterans were legally excluded because they were majority service (blue-collar) workers, and those workers were not granted access.
Affirmative Action Bill of 1961	A bill that was originally meant to ensure the employment of individuals without regard to their race, creed, color, or national origin was amended by President Johnson to include sex, recognizing that women also face discriminatory factors. Several studies have cited that White women disproportionately benefited from this policy (Crenshaw, 2006).

Teachers who embrace revolutionary love know that bias permeates school policy. They know that Black and Latine children too often miss out on academic opportunities, such as being welcomed into gifted and talented programs and, instead, are sent to administrators and specialists for "behavior issues."

This is an example of racism in schools. When teachers say, "I don't want to get political" or "I don't see color," they are being "colorblind." In other words, they are neglecting to see how Black and Latine children experience "spirit murdering" (Love, 2019) from the moment they enter the school doors through school policies, practices, and curricula (Johnson, et al., 2019)

Examples of How Black and Latine Children Are Victimized by School Practices and Policies

- Black girls are suspended and expelled from school due to their hair styles (Morris, 2016).
- Black boys are criminalized in preschools for playing, whereas when White boys engage in age-appropriate playful behaviors, it is accepted as rough-and-tumble (Bryan, 2020).
- Black children are disproportionately referred to special education classes (U.S. Department of Education, 2016).
- Black children, as early as pre-K, are expelled in greater numbers than their non-Black peers (Okonofua et al., 2016).
- Latine children are suspended for speaking Spanish in school (Reid, 2005).
- Black elementary students are routinely instructed to act as enslaved people in a classroom mock auction (Griffith, 2019).
- Black and Latine children are often treated aggressively. For example, a six-year-old Black girl in Orlando, Florida, was arrested and handcuffed for having a temper tantrum (Duncan-Smith, 2022), and a 12-year-old Latina in San Antonio, Texas, was body slammed by a school police officer (Duncan-Smith, 2022).
- Policies are created based on perception of disruption. For example, parents at Riverside High School in El Paso, Texas, claimed that the Edgar cut, a haircut worn by Latino boys and designed by a Puerto Rican barber, was antagonistic, and created a petition to ban it (Edwards, 2021).
- Black and Latine children are underrepresented in gifted education programs (Hurt, 2018).

Taking a colorblind approach will not end racist practices and policies but only maintain them. Let's be honest with ourselves. We see color at a traffic light. We see color when selecting what to wear in the morning. We see color when purchasing a vehicle. So why shouldn't we see color when we are talking about people? In fact, a Yale University study showed how some preschool educators focused longer on

Black children, specifically Black boys, when looking for challenging behaviors (Gilliam et al., 2016). So we actually do see color, and this is reflected in the preponderance of Black and Latine students who experience disciplinary action, but who reflect low numbers in rigorous academic programs. We must replace a colorblind approach with, as Mellody Hobson calls it, a "colorbrave" approach (Hobson, 2014). We must talk honestly and openly about race and ethnicity. We must understand how we are using terms related to race, and we must recognize that the social construction of race was developed in the interest of establishing and sustaining White hierarchy, power, and dominance. Race lives in our school practices as much as it does in our society. Refusing to see it doesn't help students.

SELF-EXAMINATION ACTIVITY

INVESTIGATING PRACTICES AND POLICIES FOR BIAS

So, let us begin. Take a moment to reflect on your school's practices and policies, such as your dress code (i.e., appropriate hairstyles and clothing), classroom management, linguistic expectations, referrals for gifted education and special education, behavior management systems, and assessment and testing guidelines. Then ask yourself, are these practices and policies producing or sustaining racial inequities? If so, what students are marginalized by them? Complete the chart below in your notebook to help you through this process.

School Practices and Policies	The Wording for Each Policy or Practice	Who's Negatively Impacted? How So?
Dress Code		
Classroom Management		
Linguistic Expectations (e.g., an English-only policy)		
Gifted Education Referrals		
Special Education Referrals		
Behavior Management Systems		
Assessment and Testing Guidelines		

If we are going to talk about students who are marginalized by practices and policies, we must also talk about students who are advantaged by them to get a full picture.

School Practices and Policies	What Demographic of Students Is Positively Impacted? How So?
Dress Code	
Classroom Management	
Linguistic Expectations (e.g.., an English-only policy)	
Gifted Education Referrals	
Special Education Referrals	
Behavior Management Systems	
Assessment and Testing Guidelines	

The answers to these questions are why we need to examine how educational institutions are traditionally defined by dominant, middle-class, heteronormative standards and expectations. So, instead of too often blaming Black and Latine children for failing, we need to understand how the system was never designed for them to succeed. The normalization of Whiteness is threaded in the systemic oppression in schools and, therefore, in the practices of many teachers. Now, reflect on the ways these practices and policies play out in your own work—an important step in dismantling oppressive systems at the classroom level.

School Practices and Policies	Reflection Prompts
	• What is your belief about each policy and practice?
	• How do your classroom practices relate to each policy?
	• How have your students been negatively and positively impacted by the policy or practice?
	• If your practices negatively impact students, consider a shift. What have you learned about racist systems that can prompt a shift in your beliefs?
	• Consider the practices you will shift to dismantle oppressive systems.
Dress Code	
Classroom Management	
Linguistic Expectations (e.g., an English-only Policy)	
Gifted Education Referrals	
Special Education Referrals	
Behavior Management Systems	
Assessment and Testing Guidelines	

For downloadable versions of these charts, go to scholastic.com/RevLoveResources.

The Normalization of Whiteness

Jones and Okun (2001) explain that our society and schools operate to normalize Whiteness. Those norms promote a belief that Eurocentric ways of doing things are the best ways. They are not always easy to identify because they are so embedded in our society. As a result, they negatively impact the identity development and self-concept of Black and Latine children. Those norms also uphold systems that privilege White children. As educators, it is imperative to understand and disrupt how Whiteness is normalized and how it is at the very core of systems that drive education. (White dominant norms are explained more in Chapter 4.)

POLICY AND LANGUAGE/POSITIONING OF STUDENTS

Language matters. Not only is education politicized by practices and policies, but also the very language educators use daily. Terms and phrases such as "level the playing field," "high-needs," "achievement gap," and "scientifically based" often normalize Whiteness and perpetuate cultural deficit models of students. Teachers who embrace revolutionary love not only critically reflect on their own beliefs, but also on the practices and policies that are designed to "level the playing field."

> Not only is education politicized by practices and policies, but also the very language educators use daily....Teachers who embrace revolutionary love not only critically reflect on their own beliefs, but also on the practices and policies that are designed to "level the playing field."

On the following pages, we identify "dog-whistle terms" that, for all intents and purposes, are coded language used by many educators—language that has hidden meanings that have a direct and indirect impact on Black and Latine children. Those terms—specifically, "achievement gap," "scientifically based research," "at-risk readers," and "third-grade indicator"—must be disrupted and rethought to discontinue perpetuating inherently racist practices. That's why we also include the historical/political context for the terms, critical questions for reframing them, and suggestions for what you can do to disrupt and rethink them.

Coded Language in Education

Dog-Whistle Term: Achievement Gap

Marginalized children are to blame for their lack of academic growth.

Our data shows that the majority of our Black and Latine students are not meeting state standards.

HISTORICAL/POLITICAL CONTEXT

Eugenics is the practice of White superiority through genetics. Scientists claimed that intelligence and ethnic origin were connected (Rosales & Walker, 2018).

In 1905, French psychologist Alfred Binet developed IQ assessments for children in France, which were modeled by Army IQ tests. These tests were constructed to suggest the intelligence of White recruits and the inferiority of Blacks.

Lewis Madison Terman, a psychologist from Stanford University, created Eugenics and revised the original Stanford-Binet IQ quantitative test. In 1916, he published the book *The Measurement of Intelligence* in which he argues that Indigenous, Mexican, and Black people have IQ deficiencies. He states, "racial, or at least inherent in the family stocks from which they come."

Carl Brigham, who helped develop the Army Alpha test, is the creator of the Scholastic Aptitude Test (SAT). He believed that Black people had inferior intelligence to White people.

In 1937, James Bryant Conant, one of the founders of the American educational system, called for a national testing agency to manage all standardized tests, which marked the birth of Educational Testing Service (ETS).

This idea is still used when designing standardized tests that are used in schools. These tests are often used to determine promotion criteria and have been used as a gatekeeper for gifted programs.

- See discussion about standardized tests by Ibram X. Kendi at youtube.com/watch?v=SwYiOrq5c8s

REFRAMING THROUGH CRITICAL QUESTIONS

- "What is the problem? Is there a problem with the test takers or the test?" (Kendi, 2019, n.p)
- Whom does the notion of the achievement gap oppress and advantage?

WHAT YOU CAN DO

Teachers:

- Teach students and families about the racist history of assessments. Find other ways to assess your students that are unbiased and culturally relevant.
- Familiarize yourself with options related to standardized testing.

Leaders:

- Provide professional development that examines the racist underpinnings of standardized assessments.
- Examine the frequency of progress monitoring and assessments you require teachers to administer.

Dog-Whistle Term: Scientifically Based Research

This term implies that research studies that do not employ quantitative methods are not rigorous and are invalid measures to determine the best learning program and engagements.

During a professional-development session: *Scientific research reveals that…*

HISTORICAL/POLITICAL CONTEXT

Studies on culturally relevant pedagogy and anti-racist teaching are usually qualitative studies that produce narratives about critical/key approaches to teaching based on the experiences, narratives, and student outcomes.

By contrast, quantitative research typically tests cause-effect relationships and is typically conducted with White students as a control group, and is void of cultural factors (race, socioeconomic level, religious beliefs, etc.) that impact teaching and learning. Curriculum programs that tout this research method are generally one-size-fits-all or scripted programs.

REFRAMING THROUGH CRITICAL QUESTIONS

- Who determines what research methods are valid?

The majority of culturally responsive and anti-racist teaching is grounded in critical and qualitative research practices and, therefore, does not fall under the category of scientifically based research, but it is unequivocally necessary for Black and Latine students to thrive. Qualitative research is scientifically informed and just as valid as quantitative measures of research.

WHAT YOU CAN DO

Teachers:

- Be intentional about the resources that you use, and don't just accept a program, strategy, or method because it says it is scientifically based.

Leaders:

- Purchase anti-racist and culturally responsive curricular resources. Do not require a scientifically based research endorsement, and broaden understandings of the qualitative research and the ways it informs contextual factors of teaching and learning.

Dog-Whistle Term: At-Risk Readers

(Insert student name) *is an at-risk reader.*

HISTORICAL/POLITICAL CONTEXT

The term "at-risk" came into use after the 1983 article "A Nation at Risk," published by the National Commission on Excellence in Education. Of the 18 people who comprised the commission, there was only one teacher and not one academic expert on education.

The report warned of "a rising level of mediocrity" in education due largely to factors such as student poverty and lack of teacher accountability. After it was launched, *The Washington Post* ran around two dozen stories about it, and the buzz kept spreading. This report "provided a logic for assigning at-risk status to members of demographic groups whose educational outcomes were routinely judged inadequate" (O'Connor, Hill, & Robinson, 2009). This report gave rise to the "at-risk" label that has been used in educational research that has continued to look at race and achievement. Despite challenges, such as the U.S. Department of Energy's Sandia Report (1990), which disputed the data analysis techniques used by the commission, politicians—including

President Reagan, who "gave fifty-one speeches calling for tough school reform" in his second-term campaign (Ansary, 2007)—have continued to use the report to advance their agendas.

REFRAMING THROUGH CRITICAL QUESTIONS

- How do my students read words and their world (Freire, 1970)?
- What are their linguistic and literacy resources also referred to as funds of knowledge (Moll, Amanti, Neff, & Gonzalez, 1992)?

WHAT YOU CAN DO

Teachers:

- Affirm students' identities and build curriculum around their lives, literate identities, and strengths.

Leaders:

- Reframe the way literacy assessments are used to guide instruction, especially those that rank students' reading abilities (at-risk, proficient, etc.). Provide professional learning and foster a culture that grounds literacy assessment in authentic ways to tap into students' literacy resources and strengths, such as kid-watching, IRAs, etc.

Dog-Whistle Term: Third-Grade Indicator

(Insert student name) *is not reading on a third-grade level.*

HISTORICAL/POLITICAL CONTEXT

The National Research Council makes the claim that any child who's not reading well by the end of third grade is unlikely to graduate high school and will likely have more behavioral problems in school and society. This claim is based on the notion that in third grade, students begin reading to learn, and that if they don't have the phonetic skills before third grade, they can fall behind academically.

Therefore, under the NCLB law, states were mandated to administer high-stakes standardized tests, beginning in third grade.

This claim is also related to the myth of the vocabulary gap. Hart and Risley (1992) conducted a study with 42 families and determined that children growing up in poverty hear 30 million fewer words by age three, therefore lagging behind their counterparts academically when they enter school. This research has been debunked but is continuously used to validate the notions "learning to read vs. reading to learn" and the third-grade indicator. Sperry, Sperry, and Miller (2019) conducted five studies and found little variance in the number of words to which children from low-socioeconomic backgrounds are exposed when compared with those from middle-class backgrounds. They maintain that language is richer than just vocabulary and that language environments are broader than a primary caregiver's speech directly to a child.

REFRAMING THROUGH CRITICAL QUESTIONS

- Because children develop at different rates and in different ways, why is one grade level identified to determine the academic success of students?

WHAT YOU CAN DO

Teachers:

- Teach students based on their individual needs. Support students with word study beyond second grade.

Leaders:

- Provide robust literacy professional learning opportunities to support teachers with meeting the diverse and differentiated literacy needs of students.

In Summary

Racism and the normalization of Whiteness are inherent in U.S. education, even though it claims to support Black and Latine students. Teachers who embrace revolutionary love examine how practices and policies can serve as barriers to their students and work to dismantle them. We encourage you to periodically return to the critical questions and "What You Can Do" sections in this chapter to help you do that work.

Chapter 4

KNOW YOUR LITERACY INSTRUCTION AND CURRICULUM

Teachers who embrace revolutionary love honor the literacy practices of the racially and ethnically diverse communities where students reside. They do not shy away from those practices, even if they're different from their own. They know that acknowledging those practices, and using them to inform their instruction, can bring joy and engagement and can support the teaching of more traditional school-based practices.

In essence, those educators expand their definition of literacy to encompass more than just reading and writing. For example, in Nigeria, the Yoruba people used storytelling to teach morals, values, and knowledge related to the experiences of elders. Likewise, in Mexico, many families use stories to bring life to myths, fantasies, and tales of Latin American cultures. Storytelling as a cultural practice is embedded in Black and Latine communities. It is not always honored in traditional literacy classrooms, yet it greatly benefits children's literacy development.

When teachers do not honor diverse literacy practices, students may become disengaged and disempowered. In our instruction, we may be asking them to engage in literacy practices that do not align with their own ways of knowing and being. For this reason, it is important that we interrogate our curricular practices to ensure that we get to know and understand the literacy practices from the communities of our students.

In this chapter, we share how examining curricula and classroom literature can serve as a foundation to curriculum decision-making and literacy practices taken up in elementary classrooms. We also invite you to consider how literature serves as a method to affirm students' lived experiences. Children's literature is a resource teachers have at their disposal and is important for creating a classroom that supports literacy development. We offer exercises to help you examine your classroom library to ensure that culturally responsive resources are readily available for your students—and are used effectively. From there, we extend an invitation to review and analyze your current literacy pedagogies to ensure that the curriculum and children's literature you're using reflect the cultural, ethnic, and linguistic diversity that your students embrace. Finally, we ask you to carefully investigate your own literacy journey and the ways that journey impacts the instructional moves and decisions you make daily, and to consider whether those instructional moves are demonstrations of revolutionary love or need to be modified or abandoned.

(top right) Eliza conducting professional development with teachers.

(left and bottom) Teachers examining potential books to include in their classroom libraries.

What Is Literacy?

Literacy extends far beyond worksheets and textbooks—even beyond reading and writing. We define literacy as a human right that enables us to comprehend, create, and communicate both written and oral text. Literacy is a dynamic, evolving, ever-changing process in which one makes meaning across a variety of modes of communication. It involves not just books, but all kinds of texts, including digital texts. As a society, we are adept at making sense of information from digital texts—

and our students are often more skilled digital text readers than we are. However, these are rarely considered in schools.

Children who enjoy gaming often engage in elaborate conversations with peers about story plots and characters in video games. The players use their analytical skills to critique the game design, a skill that can serve readers well as they engage in traditional and non-traditional literacy practices. The meaning that one makes when reading depends on numerous factors, such as one's social identity, time, space, and/or perspectives. Embracing revolutionary love means honoring and validating students' literacy experiences—all experiences. Understanding literacy in historical and contemporary times reveals the need for culturally inclusive literacy instruction in elementary classrooms.

Children's Literature as Windows, Mirrors, Sliding Glass Doors

Teachers who embrace revolutionary love know that children's literature has the potential to act as windows, mirrors, and sliding glass doors (Bishop, 1990) representing children's identities (e.g., race, ethnicity, religion, sexual orientation, gender, dis/ability). Bishop reminds us that children need to see themselves represented or mirrored in the books that they read. Those books affirm their experiences.

Children's literature can present new perspectives that allow readers to learn about unfamiliar experiences and expand their knowledge and understanding about others.

Just as important is the ability to see and learn about the experiences of others. Bishop also contends that "books are sometimes windows, offering views of worlds that may be real or imagined, familiar or strange. These windows are also sliding glass doors, and readers have only to walk through in imagination to become part of whatever world has been created and recreated by the author" (1990). Children should have access to books that allow them to learn from others, even if those experiences are not represented in the classroom, and teachers should be intentional when selecting quality literature. The concept of sliding glass doors points to the way that children's literature can present new perspectives that allow readers to learn about unfamiliar experiences and expand their knowledge and understanding about others.

Literacy as Historically Political

History shows, time and time again, how literacy has been stripped from people. For example, as we discussed earlier, in *We Want to Do More Than Survive*, Bettina Love explains, "Indigenous children were taken from their families and put in boarding schools that viewed them as savages. To survive, they had to let go of their language, cultural traditions, and spiritual practices" (p. 35, 2019). Specifically, she describes this as "cultural genocide." It also was a tactic for land invasion, or colonization. Indigenous culture and language traditions were inherently tied to the land and so colonialization impacted literacy. Colonization is a structure, not a one-time event, and the impact is long lasting.

TEACHING HARD HISTORY

Yet, the way colonialism is taught often presents romanticized narratives around European American colonists. Textbooks and teachings often fail to mention the atrocities committed against people indigenous to North America. The history of enslavement is also similarly "whitewashed." Enslavers are portrayed as benevolent, and actions against enslaved people are minimized.

Enslavement also inherently impacted Black literacy. When Africans were kidnapped, bonded, and shipped to the Americas, the enslavers separated the Africans they captured who spoke the same language to limit communications. This limited discussion around rebellion. Enslavers also deemed Africans as inhuman and legally banned them from learning to read and write. Despite that, many enslaved people risked their lives to learn to read and write. They gathered in self-made churches and Sabbath schools despite the awareness that "every moment they spent in that school, they were liable to be taken up, and given thirty-nine lashes" (Douglass, 1859, p. 77) because "literacy was more than a symbol of freedom, it *was* freedom" (Perry, Steele, & Hilliard, 2004, p. 13).

In the 1800s, Black people created literary societies not only to develop literacy skills, but also to counter the racist institutions that denied their humanity (Muhammad, 2020).

So, what does this mean for the classroom today? To learn about students' home literacy practices, we must seek ways to learn about our students' experiences, histories, traditions, and language. Understanding the sociocultural contexts of literacy practices and processes is an important step of culturally inclusive literacy practices. Here, we expound on this principle of literacy by juxtaposing Sanjuana's literacy practices with her school experiences.

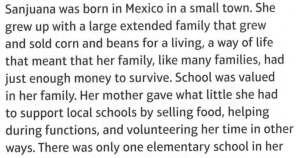

SANJUANA'S STORY

Sanjuana was born in Mexico in a small town. She grew up with a large extended family that grew and sold corn and beans for a living, a way of life that meant that her family, like many families, had just enough money to survive. School was valued in her family. Her mother gave what little she had to support local schools by selling food, helping during functions, and volunteering her time in other ways. There was only one elementary school in her small town, which was an educational barrier. Continuing beyond fifth grade meant traveling to a bigger, neighboring town and paying for schooling and transportation. Her parents knew that the United States would offer new opportunities.

Sanjuana's family immigrated from Mexico to the state of Georgia when she was eight years old. She began third grade in a school that rigidly adopted the state's English-only policy, and she vividly remembers that during the first week of school her teacher, an older White woman, reprimanded the only other Spanish-speaking student in the class for speaking to Sanjuana in their shared first language. At the time, ESOL services were offered in a school nearby. Every day during third and fourth grade, she was bused to that building to receive ESOL instruction (still in English) along with students from other schools. They were not only provided with instruction, but the

two teachers believed that students should also learn about "U.S. culture." She remembers learning about how to set a table and how holidays were celebrated in the U.S. She loved that class, not because of the instruction, but because she was able to spend time with others who shared her experiences and who were also struggling to learn a new language in

(left) Sanjuana, age 4, with her sisters Maria and Dolores

(opposite page left) Sanjuana with her mother Eulalia and her siblings in Mexico

(opposite page right) Sanjuana at age 6 with her brother and sisters

a sink-or-swim method of instruction. As Sanjuana reflects on that experience, she realizes the goal of schooling was not solely to teach her English, but also to assimilate her into American culture defined by Eurocentric principles. The practices did not value the wealth of experiences that her family instilled in her (Espinosa & Ascenzi-Moreno, 2021).

Sanjuana's story highlights what an English-only policy does for emerging bilingual students and for students who only speak English. Let us think about the latter group. What messages are English monolingual students receiving in that space? English is the language of power and those who speak it are privileged. The actions of Sanjuana's teachers strongly convey that those who speak any other language, Spanish in Sanjuana's case, are unwelcomed and should be corrected and better assimilated to American, English-speaking norms. We must think about how those messages impact children and how the effects continue into adulthood.

Now, how different would it have been if Sanjuana's teachers welcomed her linguistic identities and included her Mexican culture in the curriculum for all students?

LITERACY TODAY... STILL POLITICAL

As educators, it's important to understand that practices that are not culturally inclusive continue to exist. English-only policies are still prevalent in U.S. schools, for example. Twenty-four states still require students to score at a proficiency level on standardized tests in English to be considered English proficient (Rafa, Erwin, Brixley, McCann, & Perez, 2020). Such policies do not value students' multilingualism and instead privilege mainstream English language. They perpetuate practices that do not value the multiple languages that students bring to the classroom. As much as teachers want to say, "teaching is not political," the politicization of literacy is real. Time and time again, the language of Black and Latine people has been weaponized to prohibit access to voting, education, healthcare, and housing, just to name a few.

> We must be equipped to unpack the relationship between our teaching and politics. Once we do that, we must take intentional steps to counter the oppressive and marginalizing linguistic practices that are deeply embedded in school systems and our classrooms.

Understanding that teaching and literacy are political is important because there is a danger in remaining neutral. When we accept that literacy is political, we can incorporate multiple literacies and identities in our classrooms. We can choose to value the diversity of experiences and languages. Knowing that, it is not as easy to say, "I don't want to get political."

To embrace revolutionary love, we must be equipped to unpack the relationship between our teaching and politics. Once we do, we must take intentional steps to counter the oppressive and marginalizing linguistic practices that are deeply embedded in school systems and our classrooms. And that call is for all teachers, no matter how you or your students identify racially.

CREATING YOUR LITERACY TIMELINE

Use your notebook to complete the following task. Take a moment to think about your literate past. The timeline we ask you to create will help you reflect on pivotal moments in your life, from birth to present day, and the literacy practices that were honored in and out of school. It will also help you to see how individual practices and institutional policies played a major role in your identity as a literate being. We want you to think about your literacy practices through a dynamic lens. How did you read the text, as well as your community, your family, and your world? Prior to answering the prompts, consider the following questions:

- Where did you grow up?
- What language did you speak? What language did your parents speak?
- What texts were in the home? In what language were those texts written?
- What literacy practices were practiced in your home?
- Were you read to? If so, what was read to you?

To create your timeline, look at the developmental stages of reading and consider the questions under each one. All the questions may not apply to you, so respond only to the ones that do. The questions are meant to guide you in thinking about how different literacy practices shape your identity as a reader. As you complete this timeline of your literate life, we want you to consider the multitude of literacy experiences that you experienced growing up. We also want you to consider the many literacy practices your students bring to the classroom that may not be represented in the official school curriculum. See Sanjuana's literacy timeline on page 59.

Questions to Consider at Various Developmental Reading Stages

These stages are not static. Children enter them at different points in their development.

Reading Stage	Questions to Consider
Early Emergent *Birth to Preschool*	• What songs were sung to you as a baby? What games did you play? What stories were passed down through your family? • How did your caretakers communicate with you? • Were you surrounded by multiple languages?
Emergent *Preschool to Early Elementary Grades*	• What environmental print do you remember from your community? • What games did you play with your family and friends? • What language communities (groups of people who speak the same language) did you belong to? • How did your religious communities use literacy? • How did your family use literacy?
Early Fluent *Early to Late Elementary Grades*	• What books/authors/genres were your favorite? • Were your home literacy practices honored and valued in school? Why or why not?
Fluent *Late Elementary Grades and Beyond*	• What books/authors did you read in and out of school? How were the texts similar? Different? • Were your home literacy practices (the way that people use oral and written language in everyday life) honored and valued in school? Why or why not? • Reflect on your digital literacy practices.

Sanjuana's Literacy Timeline

Reading Stage	
Early Emergent *Birth to Preschool*	• My mother listened to music every day. She had a record player. • I was surrounded by my grandparents and parents. They believed that children should not interrupt adult conversations, but they engaged me in conversations often. • My paternal grandfather loved to tell stories, and he often told stories about the stars.
Emergent *Preschool to Early Elementary Grades*	• I attended a one room kindergarten: "El Kinder." • There were signs in our small town posted everywhere. • We went to church every Sunday and went to Catechism every week. • We were expected at a young age to memorize prayers and to be able to pray the rosary. • My dad lived in the U.S., and he would write us letters. My mother would write letters in return. • Our town was small, and everyone knew one another. Oral storytelling was important, and adults would often engage in telling stories while talking outside on the streets.
Early Fluent *Early to Late Elementary Grades*	• I had one book that was given in each grade level by the Mexican government. This book was treasured, and mine is covered in plastic to protect it. • My literacy practices were valued early in my schooling when I was in Mexico. This all changed when I began school in the U.S. • My favorite books in school were those that featured characters that looked like me. I remember loving a book about Gloria Estefan that I found in my school library. *Mi libro de primero. Parte II.*
Fluent *Late Elementary Grades and Beyond*	• I read books that were provided by the school. At home, my mother purchased the encyclopedias that were being sold from house to house. • My bilingualism was not valued at school. At school, I only spoke English. • I loved music and watching telenovelas with my mom and siblings. This was not something that anyone at school knew about. I didn't think it would be accepted as a literacy practice.

Examining Curricula

Consider whether your curriculum reflects and honors the lives of your students. Historically, as mentioned earlier, curriculum in U.S. schools has been Eurocentric and needs contributions and perspectives of groups that have been ignored. Additionally, there is a need for a curriculum that considers the lives of Black and Latine children, as well as focusing on the teaching of skills.

Take, for example, a situation that occurred in a school where Kamania has worked. Alongside Mukkaramah Smith, a first-grade teacher, she examined the recommended read-alouds for reader's workshop and mentor texts for writer's workshop listed in the school district's pacing guide, which overwhelmingly featured White characters and animal characters. Specifically, for read-aloud, data revealed 62.5 percent of the books featured White characters, 16.5 percent featured animal characters, and 21 percent featured Black characters. For mentor texts, 36 percent featured White characters and 64 percent featured animal characters. None of the books featured characters from Latine, Asian, or Indigenous communities or any language other than English. This was alarming, considering the school's student population was 92 percent Black. Furthermore, research shows that children equate cartoon characters to Whiteness (Miller, 2015).

Main Characters in U.S. Children's Literature
Statistics from the Cooperative Children's Book Center (2019)

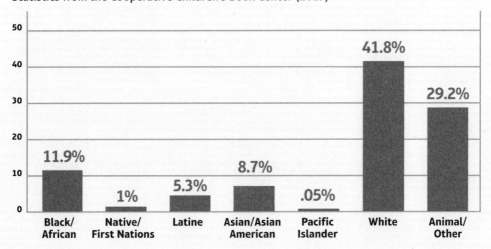

Teachers who embrace revolutionary love ask themselves, *Whose voices are heard? Whose voices are silenced? Who is missing?* (Muller, 2020, p. 5). They recognize that White characters and animal characters are overwhelmingly represented and ask, *What can we do to make the missing voices heard?* (Muller, 2020, p. 5).

The information that Kamania and Mukkaramah discovered aligns with what we know about the types of books that are published. Data collected by the Cooperative Children's Book Center (CCBC) at the University of Wisconsin-Madison indicate that the number of books published by and about people of color and from First/Native Nations in the United States continues to be scant. There were 4,035 books that were received by the CCBC in 2019. The chart on page 60 includes the percentages of characters that were represented in the books.

The CCBC states, "Our numbers continue to show what they have shown for the past 35 years: Despite slow progress, the number of books featuring BIPOC (Black, Indigenous, and People of Color) protagonists lags far behind the number of books with White main characters–or even those with animal or other characters. Taken together, books about White children, talking bears, trucks, monsters, potatoes, etc. represent nearly three quarters (71 percent) of children's and young adult books published in 2019 (ccbc.education.wisc.edu). Although the number of diverse books published in the United States continues to grow, books with animals and talking toys as main characters outnumber books with Black or Latine people as main characters. The following chart shows the number of books published about people of color in 2020. It is imperative to strive to have more diverse literature in our classroom libraries.

Children's Books About Black, Indigenous, and People of Color Received by the CCBC, 2020

	Number of Books	Percent of Books
Black/African	400	12 percent
Indigenous	52	1.5 percent
Asian	317	9.6 percent
Latine	200	6.06 percent
Pacific Islander	5	0.1 percent
Arab	27	0.8 percent

Total # of books received by the CCBC in 2020 = 3299

Data on books by and about Black, Indigenous, and People of Color published for children and teens compiled by the Cooperative Children's Book Center, School of Education, University of Wisconsin-Madison

Books help students build a love of literature and literacy. If we use only books that are mandated by the district, we risk depriving Black and Latine students of that opportunity if they don't see themselves represented in those books. Moreover, White students see only themselves in books and, therefore, are deprived of gaining an understanding of diverse experiences. This is why it is important to consider conducting an audit of your mandated curriculum.

CURRICULUM AUDIT: QUESTIONS TO CONSIDER

To help you embrace revolutionary love, we offer this list of questions to consider as you audit your mandated curriculum for bias and exclusion.

 Who wrote the curriculum? Do the writers know and honor your students' multiple identities and communities?

- Where and how are Black and Latine communities represented throughout the curriculum? Are there books about Black people that aren't about slavery? Are there books about Latine people that aren't about immigration?
- Are Black and Latine children marginalized somehow?
- Are Black and Latine voices centered? Does the curriculum suggest ways to celebrate historical figures and contributions to literature, science, mathematics, and history beyond a single month?
- How does the curriculum provide positive and rich imagery of Black and Latine communities?
- How does the curriculum honor the voices, joy, brilliance, and experiences of Black and Latine communities?
- How are the languages of Black and Latine communities represented?
- How frequently does the writing of Black and Latine children's authors appear?
- How often are Black and Latine educational consultants' knowledge used to build curriculum?

After reflecting on those questions in your notebook, what next steps can you take? Several teachers we know have taken their findings to their administrators for support, sought professional development to create a more inclusive curriculum, or modified the curriculum themselves based on need.

For example, after engaging in a curriculum audit, third-grade teacher Caitlyn McDonald noticed that a social studies standard asked students to learn about the contributions of enslaved people to the Carolinas. To address that, she worked with

Eliza to create an integrated ELA/social studies unit where third graders learned about the contributions of African people prior to enslavement and how their contributions to science, math, and history have been traditionally denied and ignored. They were able to explore how the agricultural skills of people from Barbados were appropriated when they were brought to the Carolinas via the transatlantic slave trade. Mrs. McDonald and Eliza created a unit that allowed students to engage in close reading of nonfiction about the many contributions of African people.

(top) Mrs. McDonald discussing with her students the contributions of African people prior to enslavement

(right) Students engage in close reading of primary sources (e.g., images, documents) by documenting what they see, think, and wonder.

(left) Advertisement for Sale of Newly Arrived Africans, Charleston, July 24, 1769

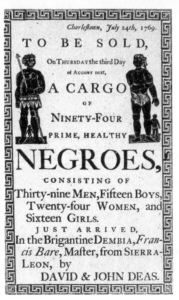

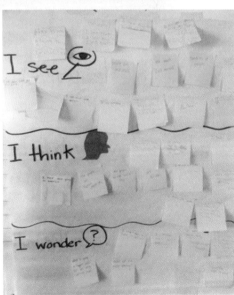

ELIZA'S STORY

At a Title 1 school in South Carolina where Eliza has worked, Mrs. Witherspoon, a third-grade teacher, asked her students to write short memoirs as part of the district-mandated writing curriculum. However, after spending weeks learning about her students' interests, communities, and families, Mrs. Witherspoon found that the mentor texts in that curriculum had nothing to do with the lives of her Black and Latine students. They included characters whose lives did not reflect their experiences.

So Mrs. Witherspoon thought and wrote about topics that fascinated her students and brought them joy, including hair. They were intrigued by her hair and their own haircuts and styles. Based on that, Mrs. Witherspoon selected a variety of texts (e.g., books, songs, poems, websites) that connected to hair, specifically Black hair, that could be used to help children write their own hair stories. (See Chapter 8 for details on this unit.)

GUIDELINES FOR SELECTING CHILDREN'S LITERATURE

When selecting children's literature to share in the classroom, it is important to evaluate it to ensure that it is not perpetuating stereotypes about individuals or groups. Use the book lists provided in this chapter, but also conduct your own evaluations of books by using our guidelines in combination with knowledge about your students and their communities.

- Because illustrations are an important part of picture books, analyze them for depictions of stereotypical portrayals of characters.
- Provide children with accurate and respectful representations of various groups and not what Debbie Reese in her *American Indians in Children's Literature* (AICL) blog describes as fun-house mirrors "that take your image and distort it."

- Consider books that are written by authors from the same cultural background as the characters in the book. Authors may be able to create more authentic characters when they write from personal experience. But since authorship alone is not a guarantee of authenticity, be sure to evaluate all literature.

Selecting books wisely can be a daunting task. But we strongly encourage you to stay the course, remembering that children's literature can be used to either sustain or dismantle racist ideologies.

Examining Classroom Libraries

If you are interested in conducting an audit of your classroom library, the first step is to get to know students' experiences and identities. Consider whether your current library represents those experiences and identities. This is key if you want to offer students books that serve as windows, mirrors, and sliding glass doors. Use these questions to guide you.

CLASSROOM LIBRARY AUDIT: QUESTIONS TO CONSIDER

- Do the books in my classroom library feature diverse characters?
- Do they represent the experiences and identities of students in my class, as well as the experiences and identities of others? (This includes race, gender, and dis/ability.)
- Do they honor and feature languages other than mainstream English (e.g., books in African American Language, books in Spanish, bilingual books)?
- Are they written and illustrated by authors who share the same background or languages as the characters in the book?

Use the chart that follows to organize your thinking.

	Tally or Titles of Books	Notes
What books in my classroom library feature diverse characters?		
Do they represent the experiences and identities of my students?		
Do they represent the experiences and identities of others?		
Do they honor and feature languages other than mainstream English?		
Are they written and illustrated by authors who share the same background or languages as the characters in the book?		

For a downloadable version of this chart, go to scholastic.com/RevLoveResources.

Resources for Building a Diverse Classroom Library

Social Justice Books
socialjusticebooks.org/booklists/

We Need Diverse Books
diversebooks.org

The Brown Bookshelf
thebrownbookshelf.com

The Conscious Kid
(Instagram and Facebook)

Latinxs in KidLit
latinosinkidlit.com

The Power of Story: Diverse Books for All Readers
scholastic.com/site/power-of-story.html

In addition to asking these questions and reflecting on answers, we strongly suggest you conduct an audit along with your students. See the activity on pages 67–70. When analyzing curriculum materials, be sure the information they contain is factual. Avoid books that depict stereotypes of racial, ethnic, or linguistic groups.

The importance of providing diverse literature has been advocated by organizations such as the National Council of Teachers of English (NCTE). According to the council's resolution, "Lived experiences across human cultures including gender, national origin, social class, spiritual belief, weight, life, and thought matter" (National

Council of Teachers of English, 2015). NCTE issued a follow-up resolution that called for classroom libraries that "facilitate opportunities to validate and promote the acceptance and inclusion of diverse students' identities and experiences" (National Council of Teachers of English, 2017).

CLASSROOM LIBRARY AUDIT WITH STUDENTS

The library is the heart of a classroom, and students need to understand the importance of it representing various groups and experiences. This activity can form the basis of a reader's workshop mini-lesson aligned to ELA standards. For example, you can embed the steps into lessons on how to choose books to read during reader's workshop. Teachers can also meet speaking and listening standards by having students engage in discussions about book choice with you and their peers.

1. **Share data with students** Begin by sharing data related to diversity in children's books, such as the data from the Cooperative Children's Book Center on page 60. The CCBC has been collecting data on books published in the U.S. since 1985. Point to the discrepancy in the number of books featuring Black and Latine people compared to the number of books that are published featuring White people and animals. Share a chart like the one on page 68 and say something like, "Let's take a deep dive into this information about the types of books published. What do you notice about the main characters?" As students share their responses, ask them what they think about the data as readers. This is a great opportunity to let students express what matters to them and discuss the importance of having books that serve as windows, mirrors, and sliding glass doors (Bishop, 1990) in kid-friendly terms (see page 52).

2. **Engage students in data collection** Next, discuss with students the best ways to collect data about books in the classroom library. You might say something like, "Today, we are going to take a deep dive into our classroom library. Readers are more likely to select books that are engaging and connect to who they are as people. I want to ensure you can find those books in our library. Let's work together to see what books we have that connect to you as people."

Tell students they will tally the number of books that represent various groups. This can be done by asking them to pinpoint and analyze the main characters in the books, and then identify them using the CCBC categories.

From there, have small groups of the students go through stacks or tubs of books, and apply the process. This may take more than one day. Students can also tally according to other criteria, such as the languages used by the authors, settings and storylines, copyright dates, and whether the books were written by #OwnVoices authors. Feel free to add criteria that you and your students come up with on your own.

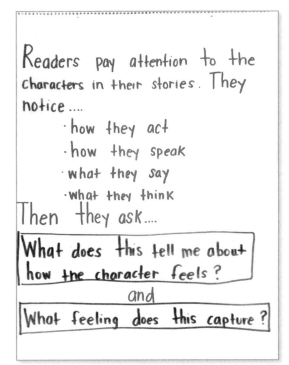

Readers pay attention to the characters in their stories. They notice....
- how they act
- how they speak
- what they say
- what they think

Then they ask....

What does this tell me about how the character feels?

and

What feeling does this capture?

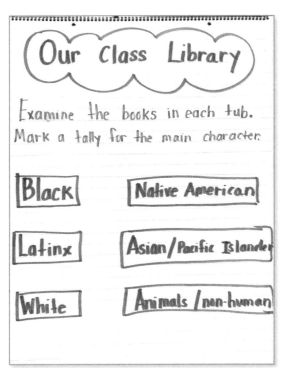

Our Class Library

Examine the books in each tub. Mark a tally for the main character.

Black   Native American

Latinx   Asian/Pacific Islander

White   Animals/non-human

3. **Analyze patterns** After collecting data, ask students to reflect on and write about the book and the connections they made. You might say, "Let's look at the numbers we've gathered and think about what they mean to us as readers." The following questions can serve as a guide for reflection and writing.

   - In what ways am I similar to characters in books in our classroom library?
   - In what ways am I different from them?
   - What groups, languages, and experiences are represented in our classroom library?
   - What groups, languages, and experiences are not?

4. **Take action** As a class, come up with ideas about how to diversify the library. You might also have students share their data and findings with administrators to encourage them, depending on results, to invest in purchasing diverse texts for classroom libraries.

To whome it may concerne, we need diverse books so we can see ourselves. We need to put diesrent people in our books. we need to represent everyone in our class. we need diverse books to learn about our colture, and honor our countrey. Basicly all the books have animal's and white people in our books and I don't like that. And for all those reason's we need diverse books.

(top) Students analyze a basket of books as they engage in a classroom library audit.

(left) Persuasive letter written by students to advocate for having diverse books in the classroom library.

Questions to Consider

Keep in mind that auditing your classroom library should be an ongoing activity throughout the year. During reader's workshop, allow time for students to discuss books they're reading on their own and ones that you're reading to them, using the following questions as a guide.

- What voices are represented in the book? What voices are missing?
- What cultures are represented in the book? What cultures are missing?
- What assumptions does the author make?
- From whose point of view is the story being told?
- What message is the author trying to send to the reader?

Adapting the Activity for Younger Learners

This library audit can be used with all grades. If you work with K–2 students, consider doing the activity as a whole class. You may also want to print pictures of the books' covers to sort them into the different categories. After sorting the book covers, post them on a classroom chart.

In Summary

It is with conscious efforts that what is taught, how it is taught, and what is used to teach it are reflective of our students' cultural, ethnic, and linguistic backgrounds. By making conscious choices, you build transformative communities where children see the humanity that connects us all. In the next chapter, we will continue this discussion of community building.

Part II

ENGAGE WITH STUDENTS, FAMILIES, AND COMMUNITIES

Chapter 5

ENGAGE WITH STUDENTS

Teachers who embrace revolutionary love build classroom communities at the beginning of the year that honor students' identities and engage them in inclusive learning. They create a foundation for learning that honors collectiveness, compassion, and multiple ways of knowing. They highlight, leverage, and build upon the cultural diversities of the students in their class (Kendi, 2018), and they help White, economically advantaged, able-bodied, and/or heteronormative students learn how to use their privilege and power for the betterment of humanity. They also do what they can to dismantle systems in which oppressive practices exist.

With that in mind, we begin with ways that you can create communities that embrace diverse cultural norms. Then we discuss ways to co-create those norms with your students. We then invite you to look at the literature you're using in instruction and offer your students the chance to determine whether the books promote the kinds of rich conversations that foster community. From there, we suggest instructional strategies and classroom routines that affirm your students' identities and honor their cultural backgrounds. Lastly, we share ways to communicate with colleagues, families, and students about how a culturally inclusive classroom is foundational to relationship building, engaged learning, and academic success.

Embracing Culturally Inclusive Norms in the Classroom

In Chapter 3, we explored the ways Whiteness is normalized in school practices and policies, but it is also important to explore how it's normalized in the classroom. James and Okun (1998) write, "Culture is powerful precisely because it is so present and at the same time so very difficult to name and identify" (p. 2).

Dominant norms are generally seen as the "right" way to do things. They are generally not questioned, even though they can hinder a positive, affirming classroom culture and be harmful to all children.

> Dominant norms are generally seen as the "right" way to do things. They are generally not questioned, even though they can hinder a positive, affirming classroom culture.

In the chart on the following pages, we explore six norms that we have seen at play in many classrooms we've visited and have even embraced ourselves. In the first column, we list those norms. In the second column, we offer more culturally inclusive alternatives. We provided some space below each norm for you to reflect on your classroom culture and to list ways it embraces culturally inclusive norms and, perhaps, doesn't. This is an exercise in identifying practices that may be harmful to students, no matter how they racially identify, and to help you strengthen those practices to be more inclusive.

First-grade students at a school assembly

Norms in School	Culturally Inclusive Alternatives
Perfectionism Perfectionism is when high test scores and grades are valued more than effort and growth and when mistakes are punished. Examples include: • Creating celebrations and bulletin boards that only highlight student work that is 100 percent accurate, neglecting to celebrate students who demonstrate improvement. • Reprimanding students for mistakes or behaviors that are typical for their age or developmental stage.	**Teacher Transparency** The teacher is transparent with mistakes, models risk-taking, and highlights strengths including ones that go beyond academics. Examples include: • Creating celebrations and bulletin boards that highlight students in writing by showcasing elements of it, such as a powerful lead, rich details, or strong reasons for an argument. • Emphasizing the power of "yet" and celebrating milestones.
Reflection:	
Individualism/Competition Individualism/Competition fails to acknowledge that what we know is informed by many others and that cooperation is key to building knowledge. Examples include: • Providing recognition and rewards for individual work during awards ceremonies but not collaborative skills or group awards • Encouraging students to compete against one another in learning instead of supporting one another.	**Communal Learning** Communal Learning invites students to work together as a team. Everyone has a job to make sure the class runs smoothly. Everyone has something to contribute to the learning process. Examples include: • Assigning collaborative writing projects where students move through the writing process together.
Reflection:	
Power Hoarding Power Hoarding makes the teacher the dominant voice in the classroom, and little concern is given to students' voices in decision-making. Examples include: • Developing classroom norms and rules without listening to the students about the ways they want and can interact with one another to learn well.	**Collective Voice** Collective Voice gives students a say about classroom guidelines and opportunities for decision-making. Examples include: • Giving students voice in establishing classroom guidelines, as well as opportunities for goal-setting and choices. They share new information with peers.
Reflection:	

Norms in School	Culturally Inclusive Alternatives
Worship of Written Word Worship of Written Word sees documentation as the only way to prove something exists. It focuses heavily on written assignments over other ways of sharing knowledge. Example includes: • Making all assignments written without providing opportunities for students to share what they have learned through other means of communication.	**Discourse/Oral Tradition** Discourse/Oral Tradition includes sharing experiences and knowledge through talking. Examples include: • Recording stories or creating digital content to capture learning; allowing time for storytelling; acknowledging that stories are not always told in linear fashion (circular pattern of storytelling). • Giving assignments that are multidisciplinary and presented in many forms.
Reflection:	
Either/Or Thinking Either/Or Thinking privileges only one correct answer and presents things as extreme—for example, either right or wrong or good or bad. Examples include: • Allowing only one correct response for questions and not being open to alternative responses, even when the student's answer makes sense and is supported with sound reason. • Seeing no gray area when it comes to behavior.	**Multiple Ways of Thinking, Interpreting, and Behaving** Examples include: • Honoring responses and interpretations of the text outside of the correct responses listed in the teacher's guide or answer bank, or your own interpretation. Supporting students with complex thinking. Examining how deficit beliefs about behavior align with dominant norms.
Reflection:	

Norms in School	Culturally Inclusive Alternatives
Right to Comfort Right to Comfort occurs when a teacher teaches social justice-oriented topics that may focus on race, gender, etc…, it is expected that it should be done in a manner that does not make White students, teachers, or others who identify with White norms to feel uncomfortable. In summary, it is the belief that those in power have the right to emotional safety. Examples include: • Discouraging students from asking critical questions or challenging content that doesn't make sense to them, and reprimanding them for doing so. • Avoiding discussions of race or historical atrocities in this country against people of color because of the emotional trauma White students may experience.	**Being Comfortable With Being Uncomfortable** Being Comfortable With Being Uncomfortable means using that discomfort as an entry point for learning with, about, and from others who differ from you. Examples include: • Engaging in discussions and truth-telling on topics related to social studies, civics, and history standards by including multiple perspectives that reflect varied backgrounds and experiences.

Reflection:

We want you to envision a classroom that rejects either/or thinking, perfectionism, competition, and other dominant norms that marginalize children. This section will help you take intentional steps to develop a classroom culture that is loving, affirming, and inclusive. The practices we recommend focus on co-creating classroom norms, suggest books that build community, and honor students' identities. These practices are revolutionary love in action!

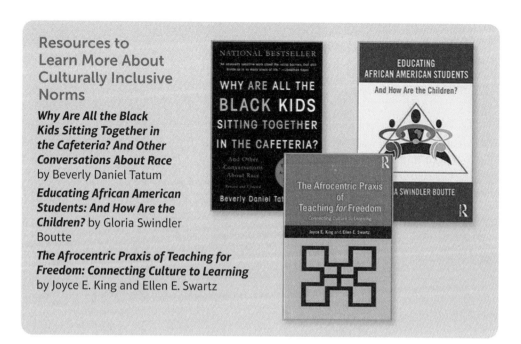

Resources to Learn More About Culturally Inclusive Norms

Why Are All the Black Kids Sitting Together in the Cafeteria? And Other Conversations About Race by Beverly Daniel Tatum

Educating African American Students: And How Are the Children? by Gloria Swindler Boutte

The Afrocentric Praxis of Teaching for Freedom: Connecting Culture to Learning by Joyce E. King and Ellen E. Swartz

CO-CREATING CLASSROOM NORMS WITH STUDENTS

Classroom norms are more meaningful and effective when they are co-created with the students. When students have a say in the principles that govern their interactions, they are more likely to follow those principles, as opposed to principles that you impose on your own. Principles are not "rules" or behaviors that should be embraced or avoided. They are ways for members of a community to engage with each other. They will help you lay the foundation for a classroom that values the voices of its members and honors its collective humanity. We recommend starting these practices early in the year, revisiting them as needed, and sharing outcomes with colleagues, administrators, and your students' families. This work is typically guided by asking students the following questions.

- How do you think we should treat one another?
- What should guide our learning?
- What does our class value?
- When someone violates a norm, what should our response be?

The norms that govern children's current actions can and will influence their later actions. When children operate in traditional behavior systems in classrooms, their actions are often met with a reward or punishment. Teachers who embrace revolutionary love know children of color often receive more punishments than rewards (Love, 2019), which does not give them an opportunity to reflect on their actions and how those actions impact others. When children operate in a community that encourages connectedness among its members, they begin to understand the impact of their actions. That is exactly what happened in Mukkaramah Smith's kindergarten classroom.

Norms to Consider as You Work With Students

- We value different voices, perspectives, and experiences.
- We can disagree, but we don't have to be disagreeable.
- We learn about communities of color throughout the year.
- We advocate (and take action) for ourselves and one another.
- We recognize and work toward dismantling oppression.
- We celebrate each other's differences.
- We listen and respond to one another respectfully.
- We ask critical questions.
- We are anti-racist.
- We are justice-oriented.

REVOLUTIONARY LOVE IN ACTION

KAMANIA AND MUKKARAMAH'S STORY

First-grade teacher Mukkaramah was dissatisfied with her school's recommended method for managing student behavior—a whole-class chart system that required her to indicate when children engaged in "undesirable" behaviors. Each time a student engaged in one of those behaviors, he or she had to move a clip to a particular color symbolizing the severity of the offense (e.g., green for least severe, yellow for moderately severe, and red for most severe).

So instead of focusing on negative behaviors, Mukkaramah and Kamania, who was working in the classroom at the time, focused on positive ones, using ancient African Ma'at principles. Ma'at principles center rights and righteousness, justice and harmony, balance, respect, and human dignity. They have been practiced on the African continent since long before colonialism. There are 42 Ma'at principles, but the class focused on these eight:

- Truth
- Justice
- Balance
- Order
- Compassion
- Harmony
- Reciprocity
- Righteousness

Mukkaramah and Kamania introduced the principles through read-alouds, providing students with background knowledge about the principles. Mukkaramah adapted the book *Light as a Feather: The 42 Laws of Ma'at for Children* by Kajara Nia Yaa Nebthet into a PowerPoint presentation and focused on two principles each day. The students discussed the meanings of the principles and shared examples from their lives and texts they were reading. After the discussions, students illustrated ways they embraced the principles in school, at home, and in their communities. See some examples of their work on the following page.

Kamania and Mukkaramah selected other picture books to explore each principle further. For example, they used *Each Kindness* by Jacqueline Woodson to explore righteousness and *The Youngest Marcher* by Cynthia Levinson to explore justice.

KAMANIA AND MUKKARAMAH'S STORY (CONT.)

They created a follow-up activity that required each student to write a letter to Chloe, the main character in *Each Kindness*, because writing real or imaginative pieces was a state standard in the district's pacing guide.

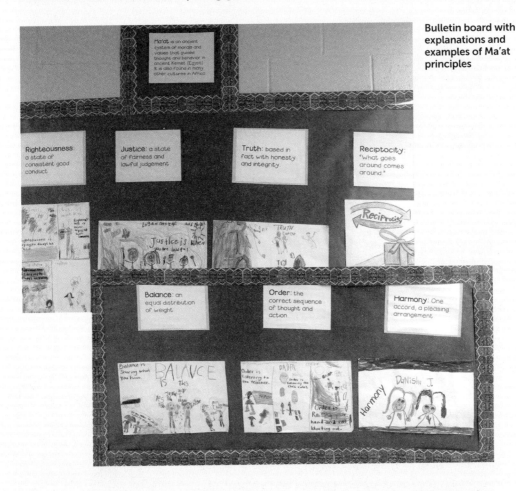

Bulletin board with explanations and examples of Ma'at principles

As her students explored books that taught more about Ma'at principles, Mukkaramah replaced the behavior chart with a chart of Ma'at principles and used them as a code of conduct for the classroom.

Practices like these create helpful pathways for resolving conflicts and encouraging self-expression. They foster a sense of communal responsibility, another Ma'at cultural principle that benefits all children.

Children's Books That Build Community

Children benefit from seeing a wide range of people and characters in high-quality literature. They not only learn about themselves, but they also learn about people who are not like them. Reading aloud to children each day provides the perfect way to share that literature and build classroom community. Read-aloud invites discussions about what it means to be a part of a community and why it's important to value all voices. Be sure the books you choose are well-written, well-illustrated, and just as diverse and vibrant as the world your students live in. We offer a few suggestions below.

All Are Welcome by Alexandra Penfold

This book features a school where children's differences are not only recognized, but also celebrated. It showcases children of various ethnicities, abilities, religions, and body types.

The Day You Begin by Jacqueline Woodson

This is a story about children who feel they don't belong and who find connections in the little things. The book begins with these sentences, "There will be times when you walk into a room, and no one is quite like you. Maybe it will be your skin, your clothes, or the curl of your hair." The book captures the sense of isolation that too many children experience.

Each Kindness by Jacqueline Woodson

This is the story of a little girl named Maya who moves to a new school. Chloe turns away every time Maya tries to be her friend, and Maya must play by herself. One day, she does not return to school. When the teacher gives a lesson about kindness, Chloe reflects on how she could have been kind to Maya.

Just Ask! Be Different, Be Brave, Be You by Sonia Sotomayor

In this book, Sotomayor writes about children with various challenges and looks at the special powers they have. She begins by telling her own story, which includes her challenge with diabetes. She goes on to feature children with ADHD, autism, blindness, and several other challenges. Each page includes a question for children to consider.

I Am Enough by Grace Byers

This book affirms children's identities. It includes simple sentences that assure children know that who they are is just fine. The book begins with, "Like the sun, I'm here to shine." Each page follows with an uplifting affirmation for children.

I Believe I Can by Grace Byers

This book shows kids that if they believe in themselves, they can accomplish anything! It is an empowering tribute to the limitless potential of every child.

The King of Kindergarten by Derrick Barnes

Barnes focuses on a young boy's first day of kindergarten. When that day comes, the little boy is ready. He washes his face, gets dressed on his own, and boards the bus. When he arrives at school, he meets his teacher and proudly tells her his name. The affirming language that the little boy's parents use is woven throughout the book.

Love by Matt de la Peña

This book is about the ways love shows up in our lives. It addresses good times and bad times, and how we must carry on.

Community-Building Activities That Honor Students' Identities

Our rich ethnic, cultural, social, and linguistic backgrounds, along with the people in our lives, make us who we are. We are multilayered and dynamic. Just as it is important to know the many facets of yourself, it is also important to know the many facets of the children in your classroom. Teachers who cultivate revolutionary love create culturally inclusive classrooms that center and honor their students' identities. In the pages that follow, we offer you engagements that will help you learn more about your students and help them learn more about one another.

WHERE I'M FROM POEMS

Where I'm From Poems is an engagement developed by George Ella Lyon in which students write about themselves and their families. When they share their finished products with classmates, they learn about one another.

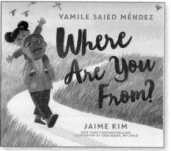

1. Begin by reading aloud the book *Where Are You From?* by Jaime Kim.

2. Introduce the idea of Where I'm From Poems by sharing several examples at George Ella Lyon's website (georgeellalyon.com) or ones you write yourself.

3. Ask students to brainstorm ideas for writing a poem, using the template on the next page to help them think about what they want to include.

4. Have students write their own poems, using information from the template.

5. After students have written their poems, give them the opportunity to share them if they would like to. You can also display the poems in the classroom and ask students to read and comment on them.

6. As an extension, ask students to choose their favorite line from the book to create a whole-class poem titled "Where We Are From."

Where I'm From Poems: Brainstorming

Use this template to capture important people, places, and ideas for your poem.

People in my life	Favorite things
Favorite activities	**Favorite memories with my family**
Favorite places	**Words and phrases that people in my family say often**

TM ® & © Scholastic Inc. All rights reserved. *Revolutionary Love* © 2022 by Kamania Wynter-Hoyte, Eliza Braden, Michele Myers, Sanjuana C. Rodriguez, and Natasha Thornton. Published by Scholastic Inc.

Where I'm From

By

malik

I am from Transformers, GJ joe and helicopters. I am from books, pincles and erasers. I am from tall, spact and playfule. I am from chichennagets, tericker and corn. I am from mom, dad and sister. I am from "be good", "be carrairfle" and "say safe." I am from cats, bags and bikes. That's where I'm from.

Examples of Where
I'm From Poems

Where I'm From

By

Intaeli

I am from Rio2, Step up 3 and Frozen. I am from P.E, art and music. I am from "I love you", "I will see you at home" and "Be good at school". I am from trees, mailbox and cats. I am from Julo Rosalia, Nathan Nathaly and Nelany me fule. I am from Tamales, Hot wings, popcorn chicken and tacos. I am from Wii, basketball and ipad mini. That where I'm from!

"RAISED BY" POEMS

"Raised by Women" by Dr. Kelly Norman Ellis is a poem that can be used as a model for a writing activity in upper elementary classrooms. Not only will it help your students become better writers, but it will also help them to get to know one another and build relationships.

Excerpts of "Raised by Women"
by Dr. Kelly Norman Ellis

I was raised by
Chitterling eating
Vegetarian cooking
Cornbread so good you want to lay
down and die baking
"Go on baby, get yo'self a plate"
Kind of Women.

Some thick haired
Angela Davis afro styling
"Girl, lay back
and let me scratch yo head"
Sorta Women.

Some big legged
High yellow, mocha brown
Hip shaking
Miniskirt wearing
Hip huggers hugging
Daring debutantes
Groovin
"I know I look good"
Type of Women.

Some PhD toten
Poetry writing
Portrait painting
"I'll see you in court"
World traveling
Stand back, I'm creating
Type of queens

I was raised by women

This activity is sure to awaken a love of poetry in students and "celebrates their homes and heritages" (Christensen, 2009). Like the Where I'm From poem, it allows students to capture in writing people, events, daily practices, events, and so forth that have shaped who they are.

"Raised By" Poems: Examples and Prompts

I Was/Am Raised by (person/people)

Example

> I was raised by
> Chitterling eating,
> Vegetarian cooking,
> Cornbread so good you want to lay
> down and die baking
> "Go on baby, get yo'self a plate"
> Kind of Women.

Brainstorm

Possible Prompts:

- What does the person do?
- How does the person make you feel?
- What is something the person says?

I Was/Am Raised by (object/place/event)

Example

> Some X tappin'
> Joystick swirlin'
> "Drive me crazy til I
> throw my controller"
> type of video games.

Brainstorm

Possible Prompts:

- What does the object/place/event look like?
- How does the object/place/event make you feel?
- What do you say or do to the object or at the place/event?

"Raised By" examples from *Teaching for Black Lives* (Watson, D., In Hagopian, J., & In Au, W., 2018)

Adapting the Activity for Younger Learners

The examples of the poems were written by middle and high school students, but we've seen equally powerful work by elementary students. Here are some ways to adapt the activity.

- Do a shared reading activity with a few excerpts from the poem that the students can relate to.
- Substitute "I was raised by" with "I am raised by" or "I am being raised by."
- Have students brainstorm people who are important to them, things they do, places they go, and events they enjoy.
- Create fun and creative descriptions using adjectives.
- Write your own poem to model for students and use as a mentor text. Identify stanzas to use as examples (rethinkingschools.org/articles/cover-story-raised-by-women)

> I am being raised by my abuelita.
> She is my favorite grandmother.
> Gentle, quiet, strong
> She is my friend and my protector.
> I love my abuelita.

Example of an "I am being raised by" poem

"HONEY, I LOVE" POEMS

"Honey, I Love" is a poem by Eloise Greenfield and a picture book by the same name. In it, the narrator, a little girl, describes the simple things she loves when spending time with family and friends. This poem is the perfect mentor text to prompt your students to share what they love and is close to their hearts, and, in the process, it gives you a glimpse into their lives and what matters to them.

1. Begin by reading aloud *Honey, I Love*, with students participating by choral reading the repetitive parts as a group, "Honey, I love. I love a lot of things. A whole lot of things like...."

    After reading the book, talk to students about what the little girl loves and ask them to share things about themselves and their families, and things they love to do.

2. Let students know they are going to write their own "Honey, I Love" poems. Remind them that, in the book, the narrator is telling friends and family members what she loves, and that "honey" is a term of endearment. From there, let them decide who they want to talk to in their poems. You may want to model this for them, for example:

    Ms. Rodriguez, I love…. [teacher]
    Daddy, I love… [family member]
    Camila, I love…. [friend]

3. Brainstorm with students the simple things that you love, taking your cue from the little girl in the book (e.g., going on family car rides and kissing mama's arm). It may be helpful to give students categories, such as what they love about themselves, families, school, etc. List what they say on the board or chart paper.

Hello, My Name is Sage.

I love my momma. I love the way my momma cook, I love the way she let me go everywhere she go.

Turn the page and see what my friend loves!

Student example of a "Honey, I Love" poem

4. Transform items on your list into a poem, following the book's repetition and cadence. Then have students try it on their own.

   You can also use the three lines of the book to have students write their poems.

   > Honey, I love a lot of things, a whole lot of things. Like....
   >
   > _____
   >
   > _____
   >
   > _____

ORAL HISTORY ACTIVITIES

Oral history is a well-established part of Black culture. Prior to enslavement in America, Africans had a rich written tradition. During enslavement, they developed a rich oral tradition that has survived to this day (Turner, 1990). During enslavement, Africans were forbidden to read and write, so communicating orally was their only way to exchange information and keep it alive. Oral history activities invite students to express their diverse experiences. They honor the Black cultural tradition, affirm the lives of all students, and help students make strong connections to course content. Here are some ways to get started.

- At the beginning of the year, provide students oral history prompts to get to know them, based on important moments in their lives. Provide a handful of example prompts.
- Have students interview a family member about a topic you plan to teach. Ask them to record the interview, listen to it in class, and begin the writing process based on it to build an understanding of the connection between oral and written text.

Building Authenticity in a Classroom Community

Providing space for students to "just be" is common in revolutionary love classrooms. Given the isolation most of us have felt during the COVID-19 pandemic, it is important for our students to show up as their authentic selves and have spaces for community healing. The strategies below will help you create those spaces.

MORNING MEETING/FAMILY TIME

The morning meeting is a great way to learn about students and their families. It is also a time when the class can come together as a family and grow as a community of learners. In the following snapshot, we describe how Mr. Valente' Gibson, a teacher in South Carolina, uses what he calls "Family Time."

REVOLUTIONARY LOVE IN ACTION

FAMILY TIME

Fifth-grade teacher Valente' Gibson believes that Family Time is an important practice— a time to invite students' families in, to get to know them, and to discuss what's happening in the classroom. He creates a community where young and old come together to share stories about life in and outside the home, and address classroom issues.

Family time begins by gathering all students together on the rug. Valente' asks the class whether anyone has anything that they want to share. Students lead the conversation by asking questions. Students also engage in conversations about conflicts in the classroom community and how they may be resolved.

MINDFULNESS

Providing opportunities for students to center themselves through meditation and breathing increases self-awareness and focus, and decreases stress. In essence, taking care of yourself is key and must be done to engage in community and take care of others. Meditation and breathing are being implemented in schools more than ever, too, to support restorative justice practices. Restorative justice focuses on repairing harm through inclusive processes that focus on community. Students are guided to recognize their mistakes, who has been harmed, and what steps will be taken to make things right (Yusem, 2018). Examples of ways to foster mindfulness in the classroom include:

- During morning meeting/family time, engage students in meditation and/or breathing exercise to help them center themselves and prepare for the day.

- Engage students in restorative talking circles (Yusem, 2018). Begin with a check-in and discuss any conflict or harm that was done. Have students reflect on what happened and what steps must be taken to make things right.

- Use the emotion wheel (Plutchick, 2001) at right to help students express and regulate how they are feeling about a current event or situation in school.

serenity + interest
OPTIMISM

serenity

joy + trust
LOVE

interest

joy

acceptance

anticipation

trust

anticipation + anger
AGGRESSIVENESS

bliss

trust + fear
SUBMISSION

vigilance

admiration

annoyance

anger

rage

terror

fear

apprehension

loathing

amazement

disgust + anger
CONTEMPT

grief

fear + surprise
AWE

disgust

surprise

boredom

sadness

distraction

pensiveness

sadness + disgust
REMORSE

surprise + sadness
DISAPPROVAL

In Summary

When we consider the cultural norms in classrooms, very little space has been traditionally provided for diverse ways of knowing and doing. A teacher who cultivates revolutionary love knows that it is imperative to interrupt and shift even seemingly harmless practices such as asking and inviting questions only during read-alouds or instruction. This can limit a sense of comfort and security, creativity, and knowledge building for students who experience learning, engagement, and connection differently in their homes and communities. The strategies provided in this chapter are a few possibilities for interrupting and shifting norms in your classroom and replacing them with other community-building practices.

 Teachers who embrace revolutionary love know when they need to shift or strengthen their classroom culture to make it more compassionate and inclusive. In your notebook, answer this prompt as you consider their lead: "As a culturally inclusive teacher who embodies revolutionary love, I am going to address (this aspect of dominant cultural norms) _____ by (action)_____ because (reason)_____."

Scholars and activists who have embraced mindfulness

(clockwise from top)
Gloria Anzaldúa,
Harriet Jacobs, Audre
Lorde, Rosa Parks

Chapter 6

ENGAGE WITH FAMILIES AND COMMUNITIES

Teachers who embrace revolutionary love engage with families and in communities, honoring students' lives outside of school and using what they learn to ensure student success.

We open this chapter with the hard lessons that Eliza learned when she made assumptions about multilingual families that she worked with. From there, we discuss how you can build positive relationships with Black and Latine families and engage in culturally inclusive and anti-oppressive practices by engaging them in a variety of ways. We identify typical microaggressions—subtle but discriminatory statements and actions that Black and Latine children experience daily—and offer suggestions for stopping them. Teachers who practice revolutionary love understand that everyone is a holder of knowledge, including students, families, and community members. So we end the chapter with engagements to learn more about the knowledge and literacy practices that exist in the homes and communities in which your students reside.

ELIZA'S STORY

Just like many first-year teachers, Eliza was excited and nervous to meet her first class and their families during Orientation Night. She posted photos of each of her third graders on the door, put nameplates on their desks, and set out enough pens to fill out the standard orientation paperwork that the school and district required of families. As families lined up outside her classroom, she greeted each child and parent as they walked through the door. She introduced herself as Ms. Allen, her maiden name, and asked if they would kindly sit down to complete the paperwork. As the parents filled out the forms, she walked up to each one and asked, "Hola. ¿Cómo estás?"

"Muy bien," most replied.

"¿Puedes ayudar?" she asked.

"No," they replied.

But when she asked Leslie's father and mother, who also had her younger siblings in tow, those same questions, they replied, "No, we're fine."

Eliza was shocked because they spoke English.

Noticing her dismay, Leslie's parents replied, "We thought you wanted to practice your Spanish."

"Sorry," Eliza said. They laughed, and she chuckled nervously.

In the early days of her first year of teaching, Eliza made a lot of assumptions about her predominantly Latine families and children. However, that moment with Leslie's parents, along with a few others, taught her early on in her career to beware of assumptions and deficit-based thinking. She assumed that because of their Latine heritage—even as a Black, female educator—Leslie's parents spoke only one language proficiently and, therefore, would need her help.

Eliza has come to define her behavior toward Leslie's parents as a microaggression. Though she intended to foster a relationship, her response was undergirded by stereotypes that operate heavily in schools. Eliza learned early on to avoid assumptions about her multilingual students and their families. When she reflects on that Orientation Night incident, as well as her own schooling that failed to teach Latine joy, brilliance, and knowledge, Eliza realizes she had internalized a belief that students and families who did not speak English, or speak it proficiently, needed her expert "help."

Microaggressions Toward Families

According to UCLA professor Daniel Solórzano (1998), microaggressions are subtle or unconscious discrimination that target members of a group based on their race, ethnicity, gender, sexuality, and so on. They can be verbal, nonverbal, or physical (Pérez Huber & Solórzano, 2015).

Multiple factors determine parents' relationships with schools. We know parents' level of engagement is directly related to their everyday experiences across school and community spaces, and microaggressions diminish the level of engagement of Black and Latine parents because they exclude and marginalize. We are unaware of any educators who intentionally send a message that they do not care for their students, yet we inflict harm when we hold every action and inaction by Black and Latine families to traditionally White standards and norms. We must be purposeful in enacting revolutionary love that not only seeks to honor and value students, but also their families.

SELF-EXAMINATION ACTIVITY

MINING YOUR MICROAGGRESSIONS

Here is an example of a microaggression that is sometimes made toward linguistically diverse families.

Microaggression	Intent	Message Received	What Might Have Been Said Instead
"Where are you from? You speak good English."	To inquire into a speaker's country of origin	You are not American. You are a foreigner.	"I am eager to learn more about you. Tell me about yourself."

- What are some microaggressions you have made toward individuals or families?
- Choose one. What was the intent behind your question or statement?
- What message was overtly and/or covertly conveyed through your question or statement?
- How was the message received from the individual or family?
- How might you communicate more sensitively with individuals or families?

Now rewrite the question or statement with revolutionary love in mind. What can you say to affirm the individual or family?

COMMON MICROAGGRESSIONS EXPERIENCED BY BLACK AND LATINE FAMILIES

The following list includes some of the ways that families and communities are described in school settings. It speaks to the subtle and unconscious ways racism manifests in the day-to-day interactions with children and families in schools, and can lead to unproductive relationships. As you can see, the left column is filled with deficit-oriented views toward people of color—views that many of us have encountered—whereas the right column contains culturally inclusive views. The language we use matters!

Deficit-Oriented Microaggressions	Culturally Inclusive Alternatives
He/she is not doing well because they do not read to him/her.	His/her family tells wonderful oral stories.
They only need to speak English at home.	They are multilingual and can draw from multiple languages for different purposes.
They don't care about their child's academics.	There are many times when families trust and respect the teacher as a professional. The parents trust me as a professional and will respond if I reach out with any concerns.
They never come to the school to check on their child's well-being.	The parents work long hours to provide shelter and food for their children.
They come from that poor neighborhood and lots of bad things go on there.	They come from a diverse and vibrant neighborhood.

Instead of espousing views that position families as uncaring or "less than," consider how a revolutionary love approach provides a different perspective and allows you to broaden your beliefs about students' homes and families.

Broadening Our Conceptions of Home and Families

When we were classroom teachers, we made it our mission to observe our students and families' interactions inside and outside of school through an asset-based lens. This was and still is revolutionary love. You most likely are, unfortunately, working within a system that contains racist policies. However, there are several humanizing and liberatory practices you can embrace that will counter those policies and benefit all your students and families. We discuss those practices next.

COMMITTING TO UNLEARNING AND RELEARNING

Joyce King and Ellen Swartz (2018) believe that cultures "hold" the needed information to engage students in learning. And to fully engage students, you must also engage their families by inviting them into the classroom for meaningful participation. You can start that by carefully and intentionally:

- observing who brings students to school.
- noticing who comes to family nights and teacher conferences.
- determining who helps students with their homework.
- finding out with whom students spend the most time after school.
- deciding on the best methods and times to communicate with family members you need to talk to in order to make informed decisions.

Consider disseminating family communication in a variety of ways. For example, you can post information in the bulletins of churches, mosques, or synagogues. Broadcast it on local media and radio stations, share with local sororities and fraternities, or create podcasts and blogs for families.

Use the information you gather to determine the most effective ways to connect with families. You might find that your students are being cared for by people other than a mom or dad, such as grandparents, aunts, uncles, cousins, and family friends. As a teacher who embraces revolutionary love, you understand the importance of being a part of the child's network of support. Your support can extend beyond the walls of the school to include other essential places in your students' lives. Engage with your students in communities that are important to them. For instance, you might:

- attend their places of worship for events such as First Communions.
- go to sporting events and dance recitals.
- shop in the stores in your students' neighborhoods.
- visit your students' homes.
- meet families at the public library or community center to help them fill out nonacademic forms.

After engaging in activities like these, use what you learn to structure learning opportunities that involve families and make families' culture and heritage central to the curriculum. For example, when Eliza taught a third-grade economics unit, she invited a student's 20-year-old uncle in to talk about his cupcake business. Students learned not only about the process of preparing large batches of cupcakes for consumers, but also how to adjust pricing based on supply and demand. Eliza later invited a host of aunts, uncles, and other family members to teach children about entrepreneurship and developing products for their customers. This eventually led to a market day, where students developed products based on the knowledge they gained from families in their communities and from the economics unit.

Your support can extend beyond the walls of the school to include other essential places in your students' lives. Engage with your students in communities that are important to them.

Culturally Inclusive Practices With Families

Embracing revolutionary love means naming the ways racism plays into your everyday work with families, and disrupting it. Eliza remembers how, each term, her son's high school teachers would send home syllabi with a final page asking her to indicate that she had read them. Those same teachers asked her on only two occasions to describe her son at home, what he liked outside of school, and what she believed they should know about him. She wished more teachers had made that request. As the mother of a young Black male, it was important for her to describe his musical abilities, his desire to become an entrepreneur, his out-of-school readings of Black authors, and his role as a big brother at home. That simple survey Eliza filled out at the beginning of the year revealed what many of her son's teachers would never come to know about him because they didn't take the time to ask.

The chart on the next page outlines school practices that often involve families. In it, we show how those practices can be oppressive (i.e., non-inclusive) or humanizing (i.e., culturally inclusive) to families. Consider how you might need to shift your practices to be more culturally inclusive.

Culturally inclusive teaching means understanding that teaching starts at home. It also means we teachers must center the knowledge and literacy practices that Black and Latine people hold. When you think back on your own childhood, you can probably recall how your world centered around your family. After school, Eliza would spend her afternoons in her grandmother and mom's hair salon, listening to women talk about the news, family members, church functions, and soap operas. In those places, she learned how to reason, argue respectfully, and digest multiple points of view through social dialogue. Yolanda Majors refers to this as "shop talk," a form of talk that occurs often in culturally shared spaces that Black people occupy (Majors, 2015).

(left) Eliza's grandmother

(top) Eliza's grandmother Daisy working in her beauty salon

	Non-Inclusive Practices	Culturally Inclusive Practices Steeped in Revolutionary Love
Family Outreach	Reaching out to families only about behavior problems	Contacting families by phone, text message, video conference, and/or class apps to share praise of students.
Parent-Teacher Conferences	Focusing on what the child is not doing	Planning student-led conferences. Focus on what the child is doing well.
Meetings and Conferences	Scheduling meetings and conferences only during the workday	Asking families if you might join them for dinner, recreational events, and/or places of worship. Allow families the flexibility to choose times that are convenient for them. Using virtual platforms to connect with families when feasible.
Curriculum	Believing that families of Black and Latine children can make no contributions to the curriculum	Decentering Whiteness. Expecting families to hold experiential, historical, and cultural knowledge that can contribute to the teaching and learning of students. Inviting that knowledge into the classroom and using it to build curriculum.
Classroom Visitors	Assuming you are the child's only teacher	Acknowledging that parents or guardians are a child's first teacher. Encouraging sororities, fraternities, Black and Latine organizations, and places of worship to take an active role in educating and mentoring students. Reaching out for collaborations when possible. Building families into curricular units and designing mini-projects where they can showcase their knowledge.
Community	Assuming negative and deficit thinking about the perceived limited resources available in communities	Recognizing that our identities are influenced by the context in which we grow up. You can create community maps to highlight significant places in the communities and have students narrate why these places have significance to them. Students can create essays/books/brochures, etc., and put them in the classroom libraries.

As an educator, Eliza knows wholeheartedly that children have stories, discourse styles, and ways of reading that can inform her practice. According to Geneva Gay (2010), teachers must learn to recognize students' capabilities that can bolster their learning. When they do that, students' capabilities can be used as "points of reference and motivational devices." Teachers who embrace revolutionary love are committed to making something of what they learn about their students. There are several practices that might be employed to build relationships with families and the list that follows is not exhaustive. However, these engagements, described briefly here and in detail in Chapters 8 and 9, have helped us to learn about our students' families and how to center their lives in the curriculum.

"NAME" STORIES

A child's name is intimately tied to who she or he is as an individual, and it speaks to the love and care that the family took when choosing the name. Thus, a name is more than a name because it holds a special meaning for the child and his or her family members. Ask students to draft "name" stories at home and use what they write as a basis for biographical or narrative writing pieces.

Name story.
MY mommy already knew that she wanted my middle name to be the same as Hers. Our middle name is Monik. I Love my middle name because me and my mom have the same name. My name makes me happy and strong. It shows personality. I am Unique and powerful.

I Intervewed my mom Shantell Rivers and here is some things She said Her favorite car is her doge charger. Her favorite game is Monopoly. She said her favorite season. is spring because it is not too cold and too hot it is warme. She said That she likes my bubbly personality. Her favorite place to go is Myrtle Beach because it is a fun Place to go. Thank you for letting me tell you about my mom.

INTERGENERATIONAL WRITING

To support young children in telling their stories and including their families' voices in other activities, ask them to interview their relatives to learn about their life experiences. The chart below captures some of the questions Kamania developed with first-grade students. You might also want to invite children's families into the classroom to share stories from their homes and histories.

1. Where was I born?
2. What is your favorite thing about me?
3. What's your favorite place to go?
4. What do you like to eat most?
5. What do you like most about you?
6. What hospital was I born in?
7. What's your favorite color?
8. What pet do you like? What animal?
9. What's your favorite car?
10. What's your favorite snack?
11. Where do you like to shop?
12. What's your favorite book?
13. What's your favorite game?
14. What's your favorite season?
15. What's your favorite exercise?

(above) Kamania working with first graders on questions to ask family members

(left) Questions developed by students

REVOLUTIONARY LOVE

Questions Children Might Ask Family Members		
• Where was I born? • What is your favorite thing about me? • What's your favorite place to go? • What do you like to eat most? • What do you like most about you?	• What hospital was I born in? • What is your favorite color? • What pet do you like? • What's your favorite car? • What's your favorite snack?	• Where do you like to shop? • What's your favorite book? • What's your favorite game? • What's your favorite season?

"WHERE I'M FROM" MEMOIRS

In this engagement, inspired by the work of George Ella Lyon (1999), you write a memoir in poetic verse, moving beyond obvious aspects of identity, such as ethnicity, gender, and age, and focusing on other aspects that influence and shape your identities, such as experiences, relationships, desires, and interests. Sharing these memoirs builds classroom community and fosters relationships, as described in Chapter 5.

FAMILY PHOTO STORIES

Equip children with digital cameras to photograph special places, people, and events in their lives to share with the class. From there, have them write stories inspired by the photos. Place the photos and stories on display prominently in classrooms and/or the school. You can even use these photos as the illustrations for books that the children create during the writer's workshop.

FAMILY READ-ALOUDS

Read-alouds help children make sense of the world. They promote the joy of reading, increase language development, and enhance students' abilities to think and talk about reading. Teachers who embrace revolutionary love invite families to engage in read-alouds. Children may also chime in with additions that add to the overall quality of the story being told. Additionally, they might invite families in to share oral stories that have been passed down for generations.

> Read-alouds...promote the joy of reading, increase language development, and enhance students' abilities to think and talk about reading. Teachers who embrace revolutionary love invite families to engage in read-alouds.

FAMILY BOOK CLUBS

Books clubs offer children an opportunity to discuss their perspectives and engage in critical discussions around text. Give families copies of the book-club books to extend those discussions, perhaps about issues of race and racism (see Chapter 8).

CLASS AND FAMILY TEXT SETS

Text sets are a collection of texts on a specific topic. They can consist of different genres (fiction, nonfiction, poetry, etc.) and media (blogs, videos, primary sources, audio recordings, maps, etc.). Find out about topics that interest your students and create text sets for them to use in class and at home to learn more about those topics.

(top) Families having dinner together after the Family Literacy Circle

(bottom) Families from Valente's class discussing the book *Brown Boy*

In Summary

Teachers who embrace revolutionary love build on the rich resources and support structures families bring to classrooms to design culturally inclusive spaces and curriculum. They see families in new ways and begin to understand the many ways that families help their children navigate school, ways that are not situated in traditional middle-class norms.

Part III

PRACTICE LIBERATING LITERACY INSTRUCTION

Chapter 7

LIBERATE LANGUAGES

Teachers who embrace revolutionary love believe that language is intimately tied to our identities. That means that, for most students, the language they bring to school is the language that they have been steeped in and learned since birth. It's their home language. It is the language of those closest and dearest to them. Children who speak their home languages are speaking the language of comfort, love, family, heritage, and friendship (Weldon, 2000). For most Black and Latine students, the language that is valued most in our society and schools, "mainstream English," is not their home language. Therefore, many of them are corrected and critiqued while at school, and in essence, denied their identities.

Honoring Home Languages

However, teachers who embrace revolutionary love honor everything about their students, including their home languages. They do not view students' home languages as inferior to mainstream English. Instead, they honor what makes all students unique, including their home languages.

REVOLUTIONARY LOVE REFLECTION

KAMANIA'S STORY

Growing up in New York City to Jamaican parents, Kamania was a fluent speaker of African American Language (AAL), Jamaican Patois, and Mainstream English (ME). She would move effortlessly from one community of speakers to another—playing Double Dutch with friends in Brooklyn (AAL), attending family events with strong Caribbean influences (Patois), and talking to teachers at school (ME). However, she never considered herself multilingual until she went to graduate school. There, she learned that the historical, cultural, and structural features of AAL had been systematically documented and legitimized by generations of linguists recognizing it as a language with a grammar, vocabulary, literary use, and history. She vowed she would never let her young students grow up without knowing the richness of their home languages.

One year, as a new second-grade teacher at a school in Atlanta, Georgia, Kamania noticed her students continuously using AAL and how it varied from her New York City AAL. So she decided to launch an exploration with the students on language. She gathered the students on the carpet and said, "To get this teaching position, I had to interview with Dr. Jones (the principal). Today I am going to act out three different versions of the interview, and I want you to tell me which one you think comes closest to my interview with Dr. Jones." Kamania then left the classroom and reentered it three times to reenact the interview, speaking a different language each time: African American Language, Jamaican Patois, and mainstream English.

After the reenactments, she engaged the class in a conversation about language, and asked the students which language she used with Dr. Jones. Many of them chose ME. She told her students they were correct, but also told them that she used Jamaican Patois

Kamania at age 4 surrounded by her father's music equipment where he played reggae music, primarily in Jamaican Patois

because midway through the interview she recognized that Dr. Jones was a *yardie*, a term for people of Jamaican origin, and how she connected with her by speaking a language the two were familiar with. Kamania also told her students that she started the interview in ME because it is considered by many to be the language of power. This sparked an exploration of AAL, the power of language, and the wonderful variety of languages we speak.

This story shows that we can honor multiple languages while teaching ME. It doesn't have to be one or the other, in other words. In the process, we can help students understand— and, perhaps, one day challenge—the power structures that celebrate some languages and marginalize others. More than a decade later, Kamania continues to teach children and preservice teachers about AAL. She finds innovative ways to weave her knowledge of AAL into state standards-driven curricula.

EXPLORING YOUR BELIEFS ABOUT LANGUAGE

Students bring their home languages to school. Sometimes those languages are entirely different from English, such as Spanish or Haitian Creole. Many linguists have argued that AAL is, in fact, a language. Too often educators overcorrect students whose first language is not mainstream English, failing to recognize the impact of that on students. This activity is designed to help you explore your beliefs about language and the language you use with your students.

1. Take a moment to reflect in your notebook on the ways you respond to students' language use. Identify a time when you have cringed at, corrected, or affirmed something a student has said in class. How did you feel? How did you respond? What do you think your response signaled about the student's language use? The template on the next page will help you organize your thoughts.

2. As you reflect on your responses, consider their impact on students. Here are some questions to guide you.

   - If you cringed, did the student notice? How do you think that made the student feel?

   - If you corrected, did the student withdraw and/or disconnect?

- If you affirmed, do you think it strengthened the student's identity or caused the student to detach a bit from his or her home language and identity? We have noticed that even when well-meaning teachers try to affirm their students' home languages, years of correction and discriminatory remarks can leave some students feeling embarrassed or confused about how to respond.

When we constantly correct or deny children's use of home languages, we denounce an important dimension of their identities. Essentially, we say you are not welcome here.

Response	What Did the Student Say?	Reflect on Your Response
Cringed (disapproved of the language use, but remained silent)		
Corrected (provided a mainstream English version for students to use)		
Affirmed (approved of the language use and offered a compliment)		

For a downloadable version of this template, go to scholastic.com/RevLoveResources.

To embrace revolutionary love, we must recognize that students make intentional choices in their language use all the time. We know children use their language to engage differently, depending on the context. They use it to communicate, make connections, and negotiate relationships. Therefore, a teacher who embodies revolutionary love must, at all costs, recognize that and challenge norms that diminish students' linguistic identities. The chart on the next page contains loving responses to students' language use.

Child Says	Typical Response	Revolutionary Love Response
"My *bruver* is going to first grade."	"You meant to say *brother*. It's not 'ver,' its 'ther.' *Brother* is the correct way to say it."	"Excellent! I remember when my brother entered first grade. He was so excited!" • *Validate children's language use and affirm that you understand what they are communicating.*
"My parents *wash* clothes last Saturday."	"You left the *-ed* off *washed*. It is important that you use the correct tense when you speak so you can get a job in the future."	"Marcus, I noticed you said *wash* and not *washed*. I love that you speak AAL like you just did and mainstream English where you use tense endings like *-ed* to show when something happened. You are bilingual, friend!" • *Celebrate and honor children's facility with language.*
"We *was* having fun on the playground today."	"That's bad grammar."	"I'm happy to hear you all were having a great time on the playground." • *Validate children's language use and affirm that you understand what they are communicating.*

Now that you have thought about how to respond to children in ways that affirm their linguistic identities, teach students to translate AAL into ME and to translate ME into AAL—to become proficient in both languages. Here's some language to help you get started.

- Marcus, I noticed you said, "My parents wash clothes last Saturday." That is perfect and fluent AAL! If you translate that to mainstream English, what would you say instead?

- Now let's try translating a sentence from mainstream English to AAL. So, if I say, "Yesterday, I jumped off the bench," how would you translate that sentence to AAL?

Translanguaging: A Humanizing and Transformative Approach

Everyone, regardless of the language they speak, shifts between formal and informal registers depending on the time, place, and audience. This behavior, known as "code-switching" (Wheeler & Swords, 2006; Baker-Bell, 2020), requires racially and linguistically marginalized students to shift their home languages to mainstream English, which happens all too often in academic spaces. We offer an alternative that embodies revolutionary love: translanguaging.

WHAT IS TRANSLANGUAGING?

Teachers who embrace revolutionary love recognize translanguaging as a humanizing and transformative approach to teaching students. When they use translanguaging, they honor bilingual/multilingual students by encouraging them to use their entire linguistic repertoire, rather than only mainstream English. In other words, as they "read, write, learn, communicate, they draw on diverse linguistic features and resources from a singular linguistic repertoire" (Ascenzi-Moreno, 2018, p. 356). Translanguaging allows all students to "make sense of a text, to construct meaning, to learn, to express, and to reflect" (Espinosa & Ascenzi-Moreno, 2021). The goal is to teach students that their language practice is legitimate and useful in any space where they're communicating with others.

An Example of Translanguaging in Action

Javon, a Black third grader in Valente's class, reads Derrick Barnes's *Crown: An Ode to a Fresh Cut* during independent reading. The following exchange occurs when he lands on a page while Valente' is engaging in informal reading conferences:

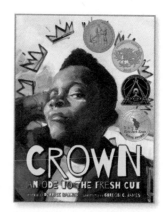

> JAVON: That barber be hookin' him up nice!
>
> VALENTE': You know they get us right!

Javon's engagement with the text and his connection made in AAL reveals his meaning making. His quick response demonstrates that Javon sees himself in the Black space Barnes depicts in his picture book. Javon is also uniquely aware of how to respond in his home language, AAL. Although the text is written in ME, he demonstrates a sophisticated skill that most monolingual speakers do not possess: an ability to simultaneously read and translate ME to AAL. Valente' affirms his AAL and responds in a similar manner.

Valente' teaches his students the features of AAL and encourages them to use it when they find it is warranted in speaking, writing, and reading. For example, one of his students, Ericka, stopped while writing to inquire if she should use AAL or ME. Instead of suggesting that Ericka use ME, Valente' invited her to choose which language made sense to use as a writer. Instead of correcting her, he urged Ericka to decide on the right voice for her piece— an important skill for any writer.

Fifth-grade student's informational writing piece on the Civil Rights Movement

African American Language (AAL)

Despite the deficit beliefs surrounding African American Language, decades of research document it as systematic and rule-governed, with its own linguistic structure, vocabulary, and grammar (Green, 2002; Rickford, 1996), and rooted in West African and Diaspora origins (Smitherman, 2006).

There are regional variations of AAL. For instance, in the Southeast coastal areas of North Carolina, South Carolina, Georgia, and Florida, many people of African descent speak Gullah Geechee—or "Gullah" for short. According to Harvard professor, Sunn m'Cheaux, Gullah was created by enslaved people from West Africa. It is a combination of their languages and English, the language of their enslavers. "Gullah allowed them [enslaved people] to speak freely, by way of encoded speech, in the presence of those holding them in bondage" (O'Rourke, 2018). Furthermore, one will hear distinct variations in AAL across the country, particularly in major cities such as New York City, New Orleans, and Miami.

Unfortunately, many educators are unaware of this long language lineage and are quick to misconceive AAL as slang, broken English, and incorrect. There is no need to teach children how to "speak correctly," because they are speaking correctly. They are

Resources to Learn More About African American Language

Educating African American Students: And How Are the Children? by Gloria Swindler Boutte

Linguistic Justice: Black Language, Literacy, Identity, and Pedagogy by April Baker-Bell

A Teacher's Introduction to African American English: What a Writing Teacher Should Know by Teresa M. Redd and Karen Schuster Webb

speaking AAL, just as other students might speak Mandarin, Spanish, or Cherokee. So instead of directing students to "say that the right way," we encourage you to honor Black children's language by affirming their use of it, centering it in the curriculum, and highlighting the beauty of AAL in the texts that they read and you read to them. It's also important to teach students to translate AAL to other languages when they are in situations that require those languages. We must understand and appreciate the languages our students speak. Let's begin building that understanding and appreciation with some history.

AAL: A HISTORICAL PERSPECTIVE

When Africans were kidnapped from their native land, they were stripped of their names, families, gods, musical instruments—anything that secured their identities as Africans, including their languages. Their kidnappers would purposefully mix and separate them during transport so they could not communicate to form an escape plan. Upon arrival to the Americas and the Caribbean, the Africans were forced to learn English, the language of their enslavers, but they retained some vocabulary, grammatical structures, and discourse styles from the languages of their homelands. AAL grew from there. Hence, there are linguistic features of AAL that are parallel to West African and African Diaspora languages. See examples in the chart below.

Phonology. Example: There is no controlled *r, er, ar, or, ir, th* in some West African and African Diaspora languages, just as in AAL.

Mainstream English	African American Language
sister	sista
your	yo
that	dat
after	aftuh

Syntax. Example: The habitual *be* represents something that occurs regularly. Several West African languages differentiate habitual action from present action.

Mainstream English	African American Language
She is my friend.	She be my friend.
They walk to school.	They be walking to school.

Morphology. Example: Possessives not indicated with an's. Both AAL nouns and pronouns often rely on the reader to use contextual clues instead of word endings to recognize plurality or possession (Redd & Schuster Webb, 2005).

Mainstream English	African American Language
Emily's pen	Emily pen

Pragmatics. It is important to recognize that AAL is not solely about language features. There are pragmatics and cultural norms to consider as well. Take, for example, call-and-response, an "African-derived communication process that is spontaneously verbal and nonverbal interaction between speaker and listener. One speaker's statement/calls are punctuated by expressions/responses from the listener" (Smitherman, 1977, p. 104). Call-and-response is common in Black culture. Here are some examples.

Call	Response
God is good, all the time…	All the time, God is good
Who dat…	We dat
Black Lives…	Matter

African American Language in the Elementary Classroom

Children bring the features of AAL to the classroom, yet often that isn't always seen as an asset. It is important to show children that their language matters—especially at the early grades to demonstrate our love for the home language from the very beginning of their schooling. In fact, Janice Jackson and Lisa Green conducted a study using pictures of *Sesame Street* characters to test children's understanding of the habitual *be* (Jackson & Green, 2005). In the study, preschool children were shown a picture in which Cookie Monster is sick in bed with no cookies, while Elmo stands nearby eating cookies. When Jackson asked, "Who be eating cookies?" White children tended to point to Elmo, while Black children chose Cookie Monster. When Jackson asked, "Who is eating cookies?" the Black children understood that it was Elmo, demonstrating their ability to understand and respond to habitual situations.

UNPACKING AAL

We invite you to go to youtube.com/watch?v=k9fmJ5xQ_mc and take a moment to listen to Dr. Jamila Lyiscott, Assistant Professor of Social Justice Education at the University of Massachusetts, Amherst, orator, and scholar-activist, as she unpacks what it means to be trilingual. Reflect on the following questions in your notebook.

- In what ways do you celebrate your students' languages?
- If you don't celebrate your students' languages as much as you'd like to, what could you do to change that?
- As Dr. Lyiscott asks in the video, who controls articulation in your classroom? You or the child? If it's you, how can you give more control to the child?

CULTURALLY INCLUSIVE UNIT PLANS

Working alongside first-grade teacher Mukkaramah, Kamania noticed that none of the picture books listed in the district's pacing guide contained any language other than English. That discovery inspired them to develop a curriculum—a more loving curriculum—that addressed state standards, while teaching African histories and an appreciation of AAL. Mukkaramah kept Kamania informed of the state standards, as well as essential questions and skills she was expected to teach, based on the district's literacy framework for students to become "fluent, effective, and purposeful readers, writers, and communicators through reader's workshop, writer's workshop, and word study." They developed the following unit plans to teach state standards from an inclusive stance.

Valente' also noticed a lack of acknowledgement of students' home languages in the fifth-grade curriculum. Together with Eliza, they co-developed a unit to teach children about their language use. The topics were co-developed by Kamania and her colleague, Dr. Susi Long (Wynter-Hoyte et al, 2021). Kamania and Mukkaramah chose the resources to use with the units that were most appropriate for the primary students, and Eliza and Valente' selected the resources that were most suitable for elementary students. The classroom teachers' goal was to situate Africa as a foundational place and space for language development for their students.

Unit 1: Starting With Self: Where We Are Geographically Compared to the Motherland (Africa)

Learning Objectives	State Standards	Materials
Students will identify the difference between continents, countries, states, through a focus on Africa's 55 countries and where they live.	**Early Childhood** Social Studies • Identify types of maps, map features, and purpose. Locate our state on a map. Literacy • Comprehend folktales. **Elementary** Social Studies • Use maps and other geographic representations to identify how migration patterns affect people and places. Social Studies Literacy Skills • Establish the chronological order in reconstructing a historical narrative. Identify and explain cause-and-effect relationships. • Identify the locations of places, the conditions at places, and the connections between places. • Create maps, mental maps, and geographic models to represent spatial relationships.	• YouTube Video: 7 Continents of the World • Maps and Globes **Early Childhood Read-Alouds** • *Africa, Amazing Africa: Country by Country* by Atinuke • *Baby Goes to Market* by Atinuke • *Bintou's Braids* by Sylviane A. Diouf • *S Is for South Africa* by Beverley Naidoo **Upper-Elementary Read-Alouds** • *Africa Is Not a Country* by Margy Burns Knight

Early Childhood Example

Assign students African countries to research at home with family members.

Unit 2: The Beauty and Brilliance of Africa and African Languages

Learning Objectives	State Standards	Materials
• Students will explore African kings, queens, and other leaders. • Students will gain an understanding of African contributions to the world's knowledge (science, mathematics, inventions, explorers, agriculture, the arts). • Students will identify African languages.	**Early Childhood** English Language Arts • Participate in shared research. **Elementary** Social Studies • Evaluate continuities and changes in cultural and economic interactions between societies in both West Africa and the Americas. This indicator was created to encourage inquiry into the development of the Mali and Ghana Kingdoms, including gold and salt mining and the connection to trade routes.	**YouTube Videos** • Mansa Musa by the Uncanny Truth • 8 Facts You Probably Didn't Know About the Richest Man in History, Mansa Musa by *Atlanta Black Star* • The Pharaoh That Wouldn't Be Forgotten by TED-Ed **Early Childhood Read-Alouds** • *Grandma Comes to Stay* by Ifeoma Onyefulu • *Jambo Means Hello: Swahili Alphabet Book* by Muriel Feelings • *Mansa Musa and the Empire of Mali* by P. James Oliver • *Moja Means One: Swahili Counting Book* by Muriel Feelings • *My Rows and Piles of Coins* by Tololwa M. Mollel • *Sundiata: Lion King of Mali* by David Wisniewski • *Why Mosquitoes Buzz in People's Ears* by Verna Aardema **Upper-Elementary Read-Alouds** • *The Boy Who Harnessed the Wind* by William Kamkwamba • *Desmond and the Very Mean Word* by Desmond Tutu • *Galimoto* by Karen Lynn Williams • *Hands Around the Library: Protecting Egypt's Treasured Books* by Karen Leggett Abouraya • *I Am Farmer: Growing an Environmental Movement in Cameroon* by Miranda Paul • *Kings and Queens of West Africa* by Sylviane Anna Diouf (part of a series on regions of Africa) • *Mama Africa! How Miriam Makeba Spread Hope with Her Song* by Kathryn Erskine • *The Matatu* by Eric Walters • *Nelson Mandela: Long Walk to Freedom, Abridged* by Chris Van Wyk

Learning Objectives	State Standards	Materials
		Upper-Elementary Read-Alouds (cont.)
		• *One Plastic Bag: Isatou Ceesay and the Recycling Women of the Gambia* by Miranda Paul
		• *Ostrich and Lark* by Marilyn Nelson
		• *Seeds of Change: Planting a Path to Peace* by Jen Cullerton Johnson
		• *Wangari Maathai: The Woman Who Planted Millions of Trees* by Franck Prévot

Early Childhood Example

During literacy centers, give students multiple fictional texts to read and summarize using graphic organizers. Also, at the arts-and-crafts center, invite them to make papier-mâché mummies.

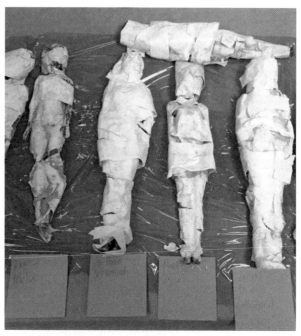

(left) Student-made mummies with papier-mâché to symbolize the way Egyptians respected the afterlife

(above) Students' completed mummies

Units 3 and 4 were developed by Eliza and Valente' for his fifth-grade students at Jackson Creek Elementary in Columbia, South Carolina.

Unit 3: Colonization of Africa, Enslavement, Resistance, and the Development of African Diaspora Languages

Learning Objectives	State Standards	Materials
• Students will examine the impact of invading countries and disrupting families, communities, and identities. • Students will be introduced to the term "diaspora" and the development of African Diaspora languages.	**Early Childhood** English Language Arts • Analyze how author's purpose/perspectives shape content, meaning, style. • Conduct shared research. **Elementary** Communicate information: multiple modalities/ multimedia • Interact with others to explore ideas and concepts, communicate meaning, and develop logical interpretations through collaborative conversations; build upon the ideas of others. • Apply effective communication techniques and the use of formal or informal voice based on audience and setting.	**YouTube Videos** • *Gullah Gullah Island* **Early Childhood Read-Alouds** • *For You Are a Kenyan Child* by Kelly Cunnane • *Freedom Soup* by Tami Charles • *Haiti: The First Black Republic* by Frantz Derenoncourt, Jr. • *Henry's Freedom Box: A True Story from the Underground Railroad* by Ellen Levine • *Janjak & Freda Go to the Iron Market* by Elizabeth Turnbull • *Moses: When Harriet Tubman Led Her People to Freedom* by Carole Boston Weatherford • *Show Way* by Jacqueline Woodson • *Sojourner's Truth: Step-Stomp-Stride* by Andrea Davis Pinkney • *Tap-Tap* by Karen Lynn Williams • *The Undefeated* by Kwame Alexander **Upper-Elementary Read-Alouds** • *Circle Unbroken* by Margot Theis Raven • *Follow Me Down to Nicodemus Town* by A. LaFaye • *In the Time of the Drums* by Kim L. Siegelson • *A Likkle Miss Lou* by Nadia L. Hohn • *Walking Home to Rosie Lee* by A. LaFaye • *Under the Same Sun* by Sharon Robinson

Learning Objectives	State Standards	Materials
		Upper-Elementary Read-Alouds (cont.) • *Africa Is My Home: A Child of the Amistad* by Monica Edinger • *Dave the Potter: Artist, Poet, Slave* by Laban Carrick Hill • *Love Twelve Miles Long* by Glenda Armand • *Never Caught: The Story of Ona Judge* by Erica Armstrong Dunbar

Upper-Elementary Example

- Have students interview family members to learn about knowledge that has been passed down in their families.

- Tell students that we have gained several ideas and influences around architecture, agriculture, cuisine, art, music, and medicine from the African Diaspora.

- Invite them to take a gallery walk around the classroom to listen to stories and view images of individuals from the Gullah Islands. They will access voice recordings and images through QR codes.

Valente's students engaged in a gallery walk

Unit 4: Introduction to African American Language and Translanguaging

Learning Objectives	State Standards	Materials
• Students will be able to recognize the habitual *be*. • Students will apply the concepts learned about the habitual *be* to other contexts. • Students will compare and contrast the syntactical features of AAL and ME.	**Upper-Elementary** • Determine meaning and develop logical interpretations by making predictions, inferring, drawing conclusions, analyzing, synthesizing, providing evidence and investigating multiple interpretations. • Quote accurately from a text to analyze meaning in and beyond the text. • Read independently and comprehend a variety of texts for the purposes of reading for enjoyment, acquiring new learning, and building stamina; reflect on and respond to increasingly complex text over time. • Engage in whole- and small-group reading with purpose and understanding.	**Early Childhood** • *Flossie and the Fox* by Patricia C. McKissack • *Honey Baby Sugar Child* by Alice Faye Duncan • Jump Shamador (call-and-response) youtube.com/watch?v=3xlgBhXfQ4Y **Upper-Elementary** • "Alright" by Kendrick Lamar • genius.com/Kendrick-lamar-alright-bet-version-lyrics (Habitual *be*) • "Bigger" by Beyoncé youtube.com/watch?v=14di5tJxn7c (Deletion of Sounds) • *Game* by Walter Dean Myers • *Jazz* by Walter Dean Myers

Upper-Elementary Example: Examining Songs with AAL Lyrics

1. Ask students to name a song that speaks to their soul or teaches them a lesson. Tell them to turn and share the song with a neighbor.

2. Have a whole-class discussion on how many lyricists and songwriters use AAL to intentionally express how they feel about life, society, and the world.

3. Select a relevant and contemporary artist that students are familiar with in your class. Be sure to read the lyrics of the song to ensure you have selected the clean version and name one or more features of AAL being used by the singer. For example, you might tell students to play the song "Alright" (radio-edited version) by Pulitzer Prize winner, rapper, and record producer Kendrick Lamar. Tell them that you like the song because it reminds us to remain optimistic despite what is happening in the world.

4. Tell the students that you will play the song twice. During the first listen, ask students to record on a sticky note which lines resonated with them. Allow them to share.

5. After a few students have shared out or you have given space to turn and talk with a neighbor, tell students that you will play the song once more but that this time you want them to listen for Kendrick's use of AAL. Students are welcome to record on the back of their sticky notes.

6. Stop intermittently throughout the song to allow students to share their responses.

7. Tell them that you noticed immediately that Kendrick used the habitual *be* throughout "Alright." Remind them that the habitual *be* means we regularly or repeatedly do something.

8. Provide copies of the lyrics so that students can work in groups to find other instances of the habitual *be*. Example: *We gon' be alright!*

9. Tell students that in mainstream English, *We gon' be alright!* will translate to *We are going to be all right!* Understanding that Kendrick was speaking directly to his community and society, he was intentional in using *alright*!

10. Chart AAL and mainstream English, allowing students to give examples from the lyrics and examples that they have heard spoken among family, friends, and community members. Discuss the beauty and brilliance of AAL and how speakers can use it when they want and how they want.

Mexican American Language (MxAL)

Mexican American Language, which is also called Chicano English (CE), is an independent, systematic, and rule-governed language (Fought, 2003). Like any language, it is the product of historical, geographical, and social events of a people.

MXAL: A HISTORICAL PERSPECTIVE

Here's a timeline that captures the evolution of Mexican American Language.

1300s	The predominant spoken language of the Aztec Empire in Central Mexico is Nahuatl, an Uto-Aztecan indigenous language.
1519	After the colonization by the Spanish, the Aztecs learned Spanish, incorporating their native language, Nahuatl. The new language is known as Mexican Spanish.
1821	Mexico gains its independence.
1848	The end of the Mexican American War marked Mexico ceding 55 percent of its land, approximately 525,000 square miles, including what is now known as Arizona, California, Colorado, Nevada, New Mexico, Utah, and Wyoming, to the U.S. During that time, many Mexican Spanish speakers began to acquire English as a second language.
1900s	Mexican American Language emerged over generations from the children of speakers of Mexican Spanish and English. Through continuous contact with English-only environments due to colonization, their first language became English. However, their English has maintained elements of Mexican Spanish with similarities in prosody, syntax, and semantics. Today, it is commonly spoken in Southwestern United States, especially in Texas and California.

Here are some misconceptions that Carmen Fought (2003) dispels in her work.

- Mexican American Language is not about Spanish speakers learning English.
- It is not "Spanglish" or incorrect use of mainstream English grammar.
- Many who speak it are fluent in English and speak some Spanish, but may not be fluent in Spanish.
- It is a non-standard variety of English spoken primarily by U.S.-born children and adults.
- It contains linguistic features that represent the Mexican American community.

Here are examples of Mexican American Language adapted from Los Angeles Unified School District's *Teachers Guide to Supporting Mexican American Standard English Learners.*

Phonology. Example: Final consonants are not produced the same.

Mainstream English	Mexican American Language
mind	mine
worst	worse
prized	price

Stress Patterns. Example: Emphasis on one syllable is elongated.

Mainstream English	Mexican American Language
today	tooday
decide	deecide
refuse	reefuse
repeat	reepeat

Morphology. Example: The plural marker(s) is dropped when forming a separate syllable.

Mainstream English	Mexican American Language
five cents	five cent
different foods	different food

Resources to Learn More About Mexican American Language

Chicano English in Context by Carmen Fought

Chicano Discourse: Socio-Historic Perspectives by Rosaura Sánchez

A NEED FOR REVOLUTIONARY LOVE

ELIZA'S STORY

One mid-September morning at Heritage Elementary School in the Southeast, where Eliza was working, the principal asked teachers to bring their students to the cafeteria. A colleague, Analise, had orchestrated on her own a 30-minute performance to celebrate Hispanic Heritage Month. As Meg, another colleague, entered the cafeteria with her class, Eliza struck up a conversation with her. Here's a bit of it.

ELIZA: Hey, girl! How's it going?

MEG: Doing just fine. So, what do you think about this right here? (Pointing toward the performance area where Analise stood dressed in traditional clothing.)

ELIZA: I think it is wonderful that Analise planned this for the kids. We teach in a predominantly Latine school but devote very little programming to students' cultural heritage.

MEG: But we're in America.

ELIZA: What do you mean? (Looking confused)

MEG: We're in America! They need to know about American history and traditions.

ELIZA: You do know America would not be where it is today without the labor of Black and Latine people. We literally built this country. Plus, we're on Indigenous land!

MEG: Yeah, but without the forefathers…

ELIZA: Well, I don't care. I want my students to stay and listen. They have a right to learn about their cultural heritage in this school, and we have a responsibility to teach it.

This was not the only time colleagues at this school disregarded students' cultural heritage. I often hear statements such as, "They will never master English if they keep speaking that slang." In Chapter 4, we describe statements like these as microaggressions—subtle assaults on students' identities and the linguistic repertoires that they bring to the classroom.

REBUTTING MICROAGGRESSIONS ABOUT LANGUAGE

We invite you to take a moment to reflect on and list similar linguistic micro-aggressions made at your school. As you reflect on them, think about how you responded or wish you had responded to the people who made the comments. After you list the microaggressions, choose one and write a rebuttal. See example below.

Linguistic Microaggression	Rebuttal
They will never learn to speak English right if they keep speaking Spanish with their friends.	*Actually, that's not true. Research indicates that emergent bilingual students learn a second and even a third language more quickly and accurately when they learn it beside their first language.*

CULTURALLY INCLUSIVE UNIT PLANS

Here are unit plans for centering MxAL history, heritage, and language in your classroom.

Unit 1: The Beauty and Brilliance of Mexico (prior to colonization)

Learning Objectives	State Standards	Materials
• Students will be able to construct knowledge of the world through exploring, collaborating, and analyzing ancient civilizations. • Students will be able to understand the many languages spoken by indigenous speakers.	**Early Childhood Literacy** • Write informative/explanatory texts to examine and convey complex ideas and information clearly. • Engage in daily explorations of texts.	• Maps • YouTube Videos: Nahuatl Aztecan Language by The Royal **Early Childhood Read-Alouds** • *La Frontera: El viaje con papa/The Border: My Journey With Papa* by Alfredo Alva and Deborah Mills • *The Sad Night: The Story of an Aztec Victory and a Spanish Loss* by Sally Schofer Mathews **Upper-Elementary Read-Alouds** • *The Ancient Maya* by Jackie Maloy • *Aztec History for Kids* by Captivating History • *A Brief Overview of the Aztec Empire* by Baby Professor • *Olmec Civilization for Kids* by Baby Professor

Unit 2: Colonization of Mexico

Learning Objectives	State Standards	Materials
Students will examine the impact of colonialism.	• Identify and analyze the author's purpose.	• Maps **Upper-Elementary Read-Alouds** • *The Broken Spears* by Miguel León-Portilla

Unit 3: Resistance and Resilience of Mexican People

Learning Objectives	State Standards	Materials
Students will be able to identify the influence of one's culture and history on others.	• Summarize key details and ideas to support analysis of thematic development. • Analyze the relationship among ideas, themes, or topics in multiple media forms.	**Early Childhood Read-Alouds** • *Danza!* by Duncan Tonatiuh • *Dreamers* by Yuyi Morales • *Frida* by Jonah Winter **Upper-Elementary Read-Alouds** • *Harvesting Hope: The Story of Cesar Chavez* by Kathleen Krull • *Separate Is Never Equal* by Duncan Tonatiuh • *Side by Side: The Story of Dolores Huerta and Cesar Chavez* by Monica Brown

Unit 4: Introduction to MxAL and Translanguaging

Learning Objectives	State Standards	Materials
• Students will be able to express an understanding that people communicate in many languages. • Students will be able to recognize and honor cultural differences.	• Explain how words, phrases, conventions, and illustrations communicate feelings, appeal to the senses, influence the reader, and contribute to meaning.	• Maps **Upper-Elementary Read-Alouds** • *Elena's Serenade* by Campbell Geeslin • *Mi Papi Has a Motorcycle* by Isabel Quintero • *My Family/En Mi Familia* by Carmen Lomas Garza • *My Mexico* by Tony Johnston

In Summary

When children speak their home languages, they are speaking the languages of love, family, comfort, and friendship. Teachers who embrace revolutionary love respect their students' languages. By understanding the phonological, syntactical, morphological, and pragmatic differences between mainstream English and your students' home languages, and the rich cultural histories from which those languages are derived, you can provide emancipatory and liberatory instruction that frees students to speak their home languages unconditionally and joyfully.

Chapter 8

LIBERATE READER'S WORKSHOP

The reader's workshop provides a framework that can help you structure literacy instruction in the classroom. While you may be familiar with reader's workshop, we want to help you think about how to implement it through a revolutionary love lens. Teachers who embrace revolutionary love believe that to implement reader's workshop, we must place readers at the heart of instruction. We also believe that critical conversations about texts should be an integral part of the reader's workshop. Ultimately, teachers need to foster a space where readers are able to use literacy to question the world and, most importantly, take action. Finally, we believe that reader's workshop should be personalized to your class. It is imperative that you get to know your readers, their families, and their communities to build a curriculum that will affirm their identities and expand their worldview. In this chapter, we reenvision the reader's workshop so that it works for all readers, but particularly for Black and Latine students.

Many classroom environments are not supportive of all readers. We've often witnessed an overreliance on generic, one-size-fits-all worksheets, which students are expected to complete silently and independently without context. This is the daily reality of many Black and Latine children. They enter classrooms in which what is taught, how it is taught, and what resources are used to teach it do not reflect who they are. As such, many of them struggle to see what they are learning as beneficial to them. These classrooms are often devoid of Black and Latine students' realities, identities, and sociopolitical understandings (Muhammad, 2020). Moreover, this type of teaching fails to present opportunities for students to think deeply around texts that validate their experiences, ask critical questions of authors and others, and engage them within a variety of genres.

> When teachers embrace revolutionary love, they strive to provide literacy contexts that not only accept, but also celebrate, readers and seek to create curricula that reflects the lives of their students.

Teachers who embrace revolutionary love know that readers enter our classrooms with a variety of literacy experiences, including a rich home language they engage in with family members, verbal and nonverbal interactions they share among friends, and many books and other texts they've received and read across their lifetimes. When teachers embrace revolutionary love, they strive to provide literacy contexts that not only accept, but also celebrate, readers and seek to create curricula that reflects the lives of their students.

In this chapter, we provide an overview and examples of reader's workshop and invite you to consider practices that honor the diverse linguistic, cultural, and social behaviors that readers bring into the classroom. We also suggest books that can be used not only as powerful tools to teach readers about reading, but also to validate readers' experiences and the experiences of their peers.

An Overview of Reader's Workshop

Teachers who embrace revolutionary love know that reader's workshop provides us with the opportunity to build upon the rich histories, languages, and stories of the students who enter our schools. In other words, reader's workshop provides an opportunity for readers to develop proficiencies in reading the text and reading the world (Freire, 1970). Reader's workshop also provides an instructional framework that fosters a reader's literacy development through whole-group (e.g., read-alouds, shared reading), small-group (e.g., guided reading, literature circles), and one-on-one (e.g., independent reading, reading conferences) teaching and learning. In effective reader's workshops, all the curricular decisions are driven by careful kidwatching (Goodman, 1978; Mills, 2004) on a consistent, daily basis. Reader's workshop also provides opportunities for readers to become critically aware of their worlds (Hammond, Hoover, & McPhail, 2005).

GETTING TO KNOW STUDENTS AS READERS

We must learn about our students as readers, but we must also learn about their lives. Observing students and recognizing their identities serve as the foundation to our decision-making, allowing us to tailor curriculum, resources, and instructional methods to best meet the needs of our readers. One way we often learn about our students' reading preferences is by asking them and their families to fill out a reading interest inventory. Typically, interest inventories ask about the child as a reader, with particular emphasis on books over other kinds of text.

In the next section, we provide two reading interest inventories—one for students and one for family members/guardians—that are more culturally inclusive than traditional inventories. Teachers who embrace revolutionary love use responses to such inventories to guide their work across reader's workshop, thereby supporting their students' experiences. For instance, when a child responds to the question about language on the student inventory, a teacher who embraces revolutionary love will use that response and validate the speaker's home language (e.g., AAL, MxAL, ME). These examples are shown to draw attention to questions we can ask that honor diverse families more overtly.

Culturally Inclusive Reading Inventory for Students

Name:

---

1. What are some of your favorite things to do with family and friends?

2. What are some of your least favorite things to do with family and friends?

3. What language(s) do you speak?

4. What do you read at home (e.g., magazines, websites, recipes, books)?

5. Which of the following types of books do you like? (Check all that apply.)

☐ Funny books	☐ Picture books	☐ Adventures	☐ Comics
☐ Chapter books	☐ Books in a series	☐ Poetry	☐ Mysteries
☐ Folktales	☐ Science fiction	☐ How-to	☐ Fairytales
☐ Fantasy	☐ Animal stories	☐ Biographies	☐ Newspapers
☐ Magazines	☐ Other:		

6. What is your favorite book? Why?

7. Name a book or story that made you smile.
   Name one that made you feel sad.
   Name one that made you cry.

8. What do you like to do on a digital device? (e.g., smartphone, tablet, computer)

9. Do you have a special reading place? If so, describe it.

10. Name someone you know who is a good reader or storyteller. What makes that person a good reader or storyteller?

11. What music do you listen to? What music do your parents listen to?

12. What do you love about your community?

REVOLUTIONARY LOVE

Culturally Inclusive Reading Inventory for Family Members/Guardians

Name:

1. What does your reader enjoy doing?

2. What does your family enjoy doing together?

3. What language(s) are spoken in your home?

4. What does your child read at home? (e.g., magazines, websites, recipes, books)

5. What does your reader find enjoyable about reading?

6. What does your reader find unenjoyable about reading?

7. Tell a brief story from your family's culture/heritage.

8. What is something that we don't already know about your child that you would like to share?

INTERACTIVE READ-ALOUD

Teachers who embrace revolutionary love are intentional when selecting texts for read-alouds. They ensure picture books provide mirrors for children to see themselves and windows to see others (Bishop, 1990). According to Espinosa and Ascenzi-Moreno, the read-aloud "is a time for the teacher to simply read a book for students' enjoyment. It is a time for us to share a cherished book and the story behind it, or a book that we know the students will just love, or a book that will introduce them to sensitive material" (2021). When working with preservice and inservice teachers, we encourage them to select texts that honor and celebrate focusing on Black and Latine communities, contain characters with strong racial identities, showcase joy, and explore activism. We are often asked whether focusing on Black and Latine communities causes us to neglect focusing on other relevant topics. And we respond by stressing that Black and Latine people are not all the same and that there is great diversity within their communities. We can read about Black, Brown, and LGBTQ families, Afro Latine communities, Black joy, Black immigration stories, Latine immigration stories, and on and on. The possibilities are endless. Focusing on a particular ethnic group does not limit the diversity of the stories we read.

> The most rewarding read-alouds are centered on high-quality literature, which offers opportunities for teachers to model fluent reading and strategic thinking, and for children to engage in discussions.

No matter the subject or storyline, the most rewarding read-alouds are centered on high-quality literature, which offers opportunities for teachers to model fluent reading and strategic thinking, and for children to engage in discussions. Here are some steps to take to prepare for interactive read-alouds.

1. **Select the book.** Think about the purpose for selecting the book. Is it to meet certain standards? To connect with a social studies unit? To cover a topic you want to address with students? Consider answering these questions in your notebook. Whatever the purpose, be sure to select a text where readers can see themselves or learn something new about others. Below, we suggest texts to engage readers in critical discussions on activism, immigration, classism, and racial identities.

   ### BOOKS ON ACTIVISM
   - *Alejandria Fights Back!/¡La Lucha de Alejandria!* by Leticia Hernández-Linares
   - *The Revolution of Evelyn Serrano* by Sonia Manzano
   - *Sit-In: How Four Friends Stood Up by Sitting Down* by Andrea Davis Pinkney
   - *Someday Is Now* by Olugbemisola Rhuday-Perkovich

- *That's Not Fair!/ ¡No es justo!* by Carmen Tafolla and Sharyll Teneyuca
- *We Are Water Protectors* by Carole Lindstrom
- *The Youngest Marcher* by Cynthia Levinson

BOOKS ON IMMIGRATION
- *Areli Is a Dreamer* by Areli Morales
- *My Two Border Towns* by David Bowles
- *A Thousand White Butterflies* by Jessica Betancourt-Perez and Karen Lynn Williams

BOOKS ON CLASSISM
- *A Different Pond* by Bao Phi
- *Each Kindness* by Jacqueline Woodson
- *Last Stop on Market Street* by Matt de la Peña
- *A Shelter in Our Car* by Monica Gunning
- *Those Shoes* by Maribeth Boelts

BOOKS ON STUDENTS' RACIAL IDENTITIES
- *Hey, Black Child* by Useni Eugene Perkins
- *I Am Enough* by Grace Byers
- *I Am Every Good Thing* by Derrick Barnes
- *Looking Like Me* by Walter Dean Myers
- *M Is for Melanin* by Tiffany Rose
- *Our Skin: A First Conversation About Race* by Megan Madison and Jessica Ralli
- *Thirteen Ways of Looking at a Black Boy* by Tony Medina
- *Where Are You From?* by Yamile Saled Méndez
- *Yes! We Are Latinos* by Alma Flor Ada and F. Isabel Campoy

2. **Pre-read the book.** When pre-reading the book, identify unfamiliar vocabulary and new vocabulary that you can introduce to students. Additionally, you can plan strategic thinking to help students comprehend the text. Guide readers to think with the text, beyond the text, and about the text so that they can gain a deep, rich, and complete understanding of the message on the page and the relevancy the message has for them and others. We draw on the work of Fountas and Pinnell (2007) in the following chart to provide more details of the strategic actions that readers take when reading.

The 12 Systems of Strategic Action

Ways of Thinking	Systems of Strategic Actions for Processing Written Texts	
Thinking With the Text	**1 Solving Words**	Using a range of strategies to take words apart and understand what words mean
	2 Monitoring and Correcting	Checking whether reading sounds right, looks right, and makes sense, and working to solve problems
	3 Searching for and Using Information	Searching for and using all kinds of information in a text
	4 Summarizing	Putting together and remembering important information and disregarding irrelevant information while reading
	5 Maintaining Fluency	Integrating sources of information in a smoothly operating process that results in expressive, phrased reading
	6 Adjusting	Reading in different ways as appropriate to the purpose of reading and type of text
Thinking Beyond the Text	**7 Predicting**	Using what is known to think about what will follow while reading continuous text
	8 Making Connections (Personal, World, Text)	Searching for and using connections to knowledge gained through personal experiences, learning about the world, and reading other texts
	9 Inferring	Going beyond the literal meaning of a text to think about what is not stated but implied by the writer
	10 Synthesizing	Putting together information from the text and from the reader's own background knowledge in order to create new understandings
Thinking About the Text	**11 Analyzing**	Examining elements of a text to know more about how it is constructed and noticing aspects of the writer's craft
	12 Critiquing	Evaluating a text based on the reader's personal, world, or text knowledge and thinking critically about the ideas in it

(based on Fountas & Pinnell, 2007)

3. **Developing questions.** During interactive read-alouds, demonstrate how to think strategically about the text. Show students how you ask questions of the text and beyond the text. Mark the places in the book with sticky notes where you want to ask questions. Think beyond traditional discussions about characters and main ideas and ask questions that require critical thinking about issues encountered in the book. For example, instead of asking, *Who are the main characters in the story?* or *How did the main character solve the problem?*, ask: *In what ways are you and the main characters the same/different? How were the actions of the main character like actions you might take to solve the problem? How were they different?*

Two Classroom Examples of Reading Aloud to Children

Reading quality literature aloud to children is one way that teachers can support their students. Reading aloud to children may take on different forms. Sometimes teachers read the entire book aloud to the children and ask questions at the end of the reading. Other times, teachers have the children interactively engage in the reading while she reads the book to them. When read-alouds honor and celebrate the diverse experiences of Black and Latine communities, all students have access to the same text so they may deepen their thinking, discuss the text and ideas it inspires, develop background knowledge, and increase their comprehension. We provide the following two examples as demonstrations of the importance of reading aloud quality literature to children that celebrate their identities and connections that they can make with the text.

HEY, BLACK CHILD BY USENI EUGENE PERKINS

To nurture their first-graders' racial identities, Mukarramah and Kamania selected the picture book *Hey, Black Child* for a read-aloud. They chose the book as a welcome contrast to the district-provided picture books featuring White protagonists. After reading the book, they turned back to key lines in the book to discuss those more deeply with the students. For example, Kamania asked the students to consider what the author means when he writes, "Do you know you can learn what you want to learn, if you try to learn, what you can learn." In response, students gave examples about not giving up on learning new tasks. Some described how hard it was to learn to ride a bike or play a new video game, but that they never gave up until they mastered the task. When Kamania reread, "Hey, Black child, do you know you are strong, I mean really strong," she paused again and asked the students, "What does the author mean by 'strong'? Does he mean physically strong?"

After reading *Hey, Black Child* several times, Kamania and Mukarramah extended the experience by making a classroom book illustrated with photographs of their students' learning. They created a digital book using PowerPoint and projected it using a digital projection system. They also printed, bound, and placed a hard copy at a listening center. By experiencing the book first in interactive read-aloud, then as a shared reading, and then independently at the listening center, students built an appreciation for Blackness, while practicing literacy skills required in first-grade standards: high-frequency words, comprehension, one-to-one correspondence, directionality, and fluency.

Terri Washington's kindergarten class bulletin board after reading and responding to *Hey, Black Child*

EACH KINDNESS BY JACQUELINE WOODSON

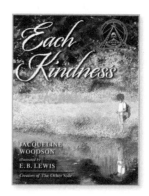

Now we will look at Michele and Sara as they engage their students during an interactive read-aloud. The students settle in and are seated in a circle on the multicolored rug situated at the front of the room with clear visibility and enough spacing for each child to feel comfortable and welcomed. After taking attendance, Sara comes to the rug with a book in her hand and sits among the students on the floor. Her presence and soft tone usher them in as they eagerly await to be invited into the pages of today's read-aloud, *Each Kindness* by Jacqueline Woodson.

This book is one of many that Sara will read as a part of her unit on kindness. Sara has been intentional in selecting her texts because she wants children to not only learn about kindness but also consider how some people are treated differently in society. While teaching this unit to former students, Sara noticed that they tended to have superficial discussions about kindness and often equated it with being nice. This year, she wants them not only to know about kindness but also to understand the structural injustices that may lead to people being unkind to others. Below is a list of questions that Sara asked before, during, and after reading the book.

Questions Sara Posed Before, During, After Her Read-Aloud		
Before	**During**	**After**
• What does it mean to be kind? • What are some reasons why some people choose not to be kind?	• Why do you think the girls didn't want to play with Maya? • Why does Chloe want Maya to come back to school?	• Why do you think the other kids were not very nice to the new girl, Maya? • How do you think Maya felt? How did she react to their unkindness? • Was Maya's treatment fair? • What could the students have done differently to be kind?

Sara is intentional about the questions she asks while reading *Each Kindness*. Before any read-aloud, she prepares by reading the book closely and writing questions on sticky notes. She also writes questions to discuss after the reading on an anchor chart, which gives students the opportunity to think about them while she is reading.

Sara's questions help students think critically about the text. Some, for example, encourage students to think about why no one played with Maya. Other questions cause them to consider whether social class played a role in the students not wanting to play with Maya.

This is more than a read-aloud. It is an intentionally designed experience that Michele and Sara carry out regularly to support and engage readers. Sara pushes the discussion beyond events in the text to what they mean in her students' lives. Sara doesn't rush students to finish what they're saying, nor does she listen only to the one or two most vocal children. She allows all children who wish to speak to do so. She doesn't privilege some voices, nor allow some voices to dominate the discussion. Sara speaks only to encourage the children to elaborate on a comment or to ask another question.

Sara reading aloud a picture book during the kindness unit

MINI-LESSONS

Reading mini-lessons are instrumental in helping readers become strategic thinkers. Although they are brief, they are powerful because they focus on principles that will support students' independent reading behaviors and reading processes. They support readers in thinking strategically and allow teachers to demonstrate those behaviors and processes. They also allow teachers to use their knowledge about students' lives to choose books to share. Begin each mini-lesson with a brief statement about the behavior or process you're going to teach. Let students know what they need to do and how it will help to make them better readers. Here are some examples.

> Although they are brief, mini-lessons are powerful because they focus on principles that will support students' independent reading behaviors and reading processes.

Reading Mini-Lesson: Reading Is Thinking

Reading is thinking. Yesterday, we discussed how readers think as they read. They may…

- Summarize
- Infer (This means… because…)
- Question (I wonder…)
- Visualize (I can see… as I read…)
- Make connections (This book reminds me of…)
- Make predictions (I believe… will happen next because…)

Two Classroom Examples of Mini-Lessons

Mini-lessons provide powerful demonstrations for readers to learn more about the strategic thinking that proficient readers engage in when reading. You can integrate many mini-lessons across the year into your reader's workshops. Mini-lessons should not be long and laborious, but brief, explicit demonstrations for your readers. As such, we provide two examples of mini-lessons for you to consider.

Thinking Deeply About Text

In this example, the teacher gives students the opportunity to jot down their thinking as readers, using prompts such these:

- What did you learn?
- Surprises (I am surprised...)
- Questions (How? Why? When? Where?)
- Comparisons and contrasts (This reminds me of...)
- Questions (I wonder...)

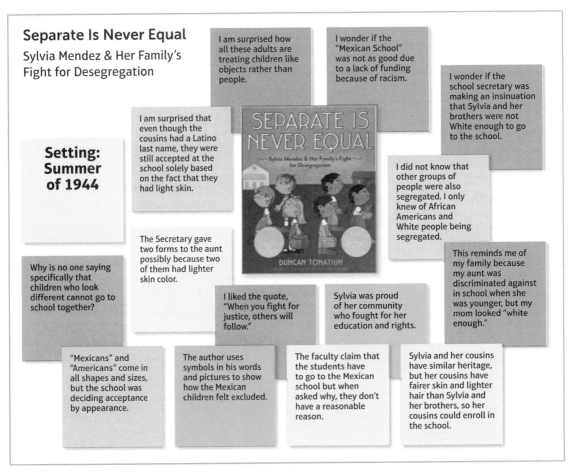

Separate Is Never Equal
Sylvia Mendez & Her Family's Fight for Desegregation

I am surprised how all these adults are treating children like objects rather than people.

I wonder if the "Mexican School" was not as good due to a lack of funding because of racism.

I wonder if the school secretary was making an insinuation that Sylvia and her brothers were not White enough to go to the school.

I am surprised that even though the cousins had a Latino last name, they were still accepted at the school solely based on the fact that they had light skin.

Setting: Summer of 1944

I did not know that other groups of people were also segregated. I only knew of African Americans and White people being segregated.

The Secretary gave two forms to the aunt possibly because two of them had lighter skin color.

Why is no one saying specifically that children who look different cannot go to school together?

This reminds me of my family because my aunt was discriminated against in school when she was younger, but my mom looked "white enough."

I liked the quote, "When you fight for justice, others will follow."

Sylvia was proud of her community who fought for her education and rights.

"Mexicans" and "Americans" come in all shapes and sizes, but the school was deciding acceptance by appearance.

The author uses symbols in his words and pictures to show how the Mexican children felt excluded.

The faculty claim that the students have to go to the Mexican school but when asked why, they don't have a reasonable reason.

Sylvia and her cousins have similar heritage, but her cousins have fairer skin and lighter hair than Sylvia and her brothers, so her cousins could enroll in the school.

A jamboard based on students' reading of Duncan Tonatiuh's *Separate Is Never Equal: Sylvia Mendez & Her Family's Fight for Desegregation*

During these lessons, the teacher is very intentional in using texts by Black and Latine children's book authors. She also offers a variety of digital formats for responding (e.g., jamboards, blogs, digital reader's notebooks). She shares powerful statements about what readers do and how they think, specifically, by using what she knows about students' interests and referencing topics they have shared in their Where I'm From Poems (see pages 83–85 for details).

Determining a Character's Feelings

In this example, the teacher provides a mini-lesson on determining a character's feelings.

1. **Connect:** *Yesterday, we talked about how reading is thinking. When we are reading fictional stories, we are always thinking about the characters because they are so important to a story. Can you imagine the story* Black Panther *without the main character T'Challa?*

   Today you'll learn that one way we get to know characters well is to make sure we understand how they feel, talk, act, and think. Then, we can find the right words to describe that feeling.

   What are some feelings we experience? Students may say happiness, sadness, excitement, shock, fear, surprise, sleepiness, disappointment, disgust, worry, anger, confusion, nervousness, loneliness, boredom, and/or jealousy.

2. **Teach:** *Watch how I use clues from what a character does, what she says, and what she thinks to find the right word to describe her feelings. Remember, this will help understand the character better.*

   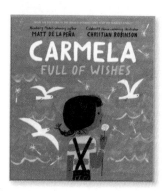

   Develop an anchor chart with students based on *Carmela, Full of Wishes* by Matt De la Peña (2018).

3. **Active Engagement:** Put students in small groups and give each group some sticky notes and a book you have read aloud to the whole class. *I have given each group a book we've read together. On each page, I want you to think about the main character's actions, how she or he speaks, what she or he says, and what she or he thinks. Use sticky notes to capture your thoughts in the book.*

   Then select one word to describe how the character feels.

   From there, create one sentence to describe the character's feeling, using this frame:

_____ feels _____ because _____.		
(character)	(feeling)	(action, language, thinking)

   Example: Carmela's brother feels annoyed because he glared and snapped at Carmela when she spoke to him.

4. **Link:** *Today and every day, during independent reading, imagine how your characters are feeling and name that feeling. Remember to think about characters' actions, how they speak, what they say, and what they think. As you are reading independently, write the feeling of your main character on a sticky note to share with others.*

   When a teacher who embraces revolutionary love gives this lesson, she notices how her students describe an individual's feelings from movies, cartoons, and even stories they share about things that have occurred at home and in their community. She is mindful to use that knowledge to help students make text-to-self, text-to-text, and text-to-world connections. For example, several children have commented on their love of Black Panther, a superhero in Marvel Comics. As a result, she references the character during the mini-lesson, and often invites kids to analyze popular movies, commercials, and characters in stories that matter to them.

At the end of each mini-lesson, after students have tried to apply the strategy to their own work, be sure to let them share their work. Next, we dig into independent reading and the intentional moves teachers make to support readers in revolutionary loving ways.

INDEPENDENT READING

Children become proficient readers when they are critical consumers of texts. Following your interactive read-aloud, consider engaging students in independent reading. Independent reading provides an opportunity for children to select books that interest them and to try out the strategies that they've learned from you during whole-group, small-group, and one-on-one instruction. During independent reading, students read books on their own while you hold individual conferences. To help keep their book selection organized, you might give them Browse Bags—curated collections of materials from the classroom library that they read during independent reading (Myers, 2019). You can use the information that you learn from each reader to carefully select the materials that will go in the Browse Bags. The ultimate goal is for readers to have materials that they can read and want to read.

Teachers who embrace revolutionary love understand the importance of building a diverse classroom library (see Chapter 3) based on what they have come to learn about their students, families, and the community (see Chapter 5). They urge their students to select books that will pique their interests and support them as readers by providing access to a wide selection of books, without hemming in students by leveled texts.

One-to-one reading conferences between teacher and student are at the heart of independent reading. When conferring with students, help them move beyond just picking books to add to their bags to thinking about their rationale for choosing each book. The reading conference lets you get to know students as readers; it also allows students to know that they are a part of a reading community. During conference time, engage students in a discussion to find out what they are reading, encourage students to think about other books they may read, and help students set goals for themselves as readers. As you confer with students, always consider this question: What does this reader need? This will help you as you plan instruction to support your readers. Be open to learning about your students, their lives, and their reading preferences. Questions like these will help:

- What are you reading?
- What do you need to help you become a better reader?
- What topics are you interested in learning more about?

Encourage Children to Read Expansively

Teachers who embrace revolutionary love encourage readers to engage with a variety of texts during reader's workshop. Text types might include poems, speeches, child-friendly song lyrics, bilingual books, recipes, books made by and with their classmates, and several other possibilities. For example, when Eliza was a classroom teacher, she noticed one of her students, Arelia, reading a piece of paper each morning. One day, Eliza asked Arelia about it. Arelia explained that she was learning her prayers in preparation for her First Holy Communion, a Catholic devotion ceremony, an event that was special and meaningful to her. Eliza invited Arelia to add her prayers to her Browse Bag. It was important that Arelia understood that her church literacies were valid at school. Eliza made a point to ask questions about Arelia's reading of the prayers, and was excited when she eventually attended Arelia's First Communion as a guest.

Reading Assessment Through a Revolutionary Love Lens

Ongoing assessment is a critical part of teaching readers, and independent reading is the perfect time to carry it out with individual students. The goals of assessment are myriad, including:

- to learn about students as literate beings (Paley, 2000; Serravallo, 2019).
- to create curriculum for and with them.
- to group them for guided reading, reading strategy lessons, and individualized instruction.
- to determine their strengths and areas of growth.

KIDWATCHING AND NOTE-TAKING

If we return to Sara's classroom, we notice that she and Michele sit side by side with students, taking kidwatching notes on a clipboard (Goodman, 1978; Mills, 2004). Their notes may include observations about what the child says and does as a reader, an oral reading record of the child's use of the cueing system (Ascenzi-Moreno, 2018; Briceño & Klein, 2019; Clay 1991), and evidence of the child's strategic meaning-making processes.

A teacher who embraces revolutionary love understands that students bring cultural references that support meaning-making when reading. When listening to children read, you may notice they deviate from the text, something that *all* readers do, even proficient readers. Each time a child misreads the text, it serves as a window into the sources of information he or she is using. We don't consider a child's misreadings, or miscues, as errors, but rather as information to help us support him or her. As reading teachers, our goal is to help students make sense of the text.

When we assess and confer with students, we want to understand *all* the information they are using as readers, including word-level information. We should be aware of the strategies that support them in applying their alphabet knowledge and what they have learned from your phonological awareness, phonics, and spelling lessons as they engage with authentic texts that we have recommended throughout this book. We believe that explicit phonics and phonological awareness should be taught. However, they should be taught in the context of real reading and real writing. We teach phonics through a whole-part-whole method (Strickland, 1998). For example, when a student is reading a text and comes to a word he or she doesn't know, we teach the child to use phonics to decode the word, and then ask him or her to use the word in meaningful contexts, considering the cultural references and background knowledge that support students around meaning-making.

Prompts to Consider When Listening to Students Read

- What happened in the story when…?
- What word would make sense here?
- Think about something like this that happened to you.
- How is the text structured?
- What word sounds right?
- What is another word that might fit here?
- Look at the first letter. What sound does it make? What comes next?
- What would make sense?
- Look at the beginning of the word. Is there a letter (or letters) that sound like your word?
- Look at the end of the word.
- Do you see any chunks in the word that are like chunks in other words you know?

Let's look at Michele's notebook, which contains data on Christian, a Black male emerging reader.

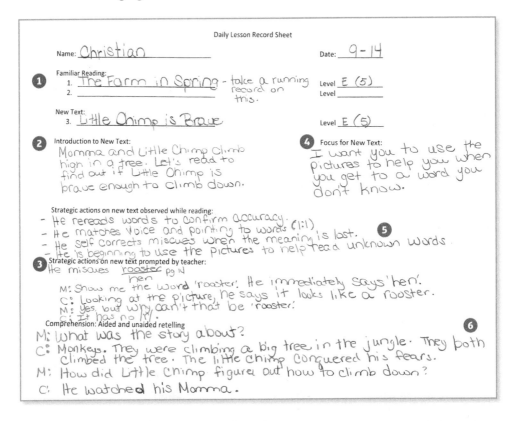

Daily Lesson Record Sheet

Name: Christian   Date: 9-14

1 Familiar Reading:
 1. The Farm in Spring - take a running record on this.   Level E (5)
 2. _____   Level _____

New Text:
 3. Little Chimp is Brave   Level E (5)

2 Introduction to New Text:
Momma and Little Chimp climb high in a tree. Let's read to find out if Little Chimp is brave enough to climb down.

4 Focus for New Text:
I want you to use the pictures to help you when you get to a word you don't know.

Strategic actions on new text observed while reading:
- He rereads words to confirm accuracy.
- He matches voice and pointing to words (1:1).
- He self corrects miscues when the meaning is lost.
- He is beginning to use the pictures to help read unknown words.   **5**

3 Strategic actions on new text prompted by teacher:
He miscues rooster pg 14
              hen
M: Show me the word 'rooster'. He immediately says 'hen'.
C: Looking at the picture, he says it looks like a rooster.
M: Yes, but why can't that be 'rooster'.
C: It has no /r/.

Comprehension: Aided and unaided retelling   **6**
M: What was the story about?
C: Monkeys. They were climbing a big tree in the jungle. They both climbed the tree. The little chimp conquered his fears.
M: How did Little Chimp figure out how to climb down?
C: He watched his Momma.

1 Michele collects kidwatching data on Christian on the Daily Lesson Sheet when she works with him one-on-one. She begins by having Christian read a familiar book from his Browse Bag. These are books that Christian has read before with Michele. Having him reread these familiar texts builds fluency. Michele will take a running record on this book.

2 Michele then introduces the new book that Christian will read. She carefully selects this book based on reading strategies that her previous data on Christian reveals he still needs to work on. Michele introduces the new book, sets the focus strategy for Christian to try, and then observes the strategic actions he uses when reading.

3 When Christian reads the familiar text, he makes several miscues. To help Christian practice cross-checking semantic and graphophonemic cues, the focus of this lesson, Michele asks Christian to show her the word *rooster*. She wants to see if he will understand that while the picture may look like a rooster, the word in the text is actually *hen*. He figures it out.

4 Based on previous data, Michele wants Christian to practice cross-checking cues when he makes an attempt at reading an unknown word.

5 From this observation, Michele has data that Christian is employing effective strategic actions when reading. For instance, he corrects his miscues when they do not make sense, and he rereads to confirm accuracy.

6 To check his understanding of the new story he just read, Michele asks Christian to tell her what the story was about. He is able to provide an accurate retelling.

7 Writing:

He dictates this sentence below.

Message Composed:

(I) (go) (to) (the) store to buy ~~me~~ am (two) roses.

Cut Up Story, Space Concepts Sequence, Phrasing

8 Words Spelled Correctly _____ 5

Phonemes correctly identified _____ 8

He writes this in his journal.

| I | go | to | the | stor | to |
| b | am | two | rose |

9 Letter Work, Breaking Words, Word Work and Analysis

I gave him magnetic letters to make words that rhymes with 'hen'. He was able to make and read hen ten den men pen

Constructing Words, Gaining Fluency

10 General Comments on Lesson:

He still needs to work on cross checking cues to make a guess at unknow words. Have him look at the picture and the beginning letter of the unknown word to make a guess.

7 Michele then asks Christian what he'd like to write in his journal. The goal is to help him understand that spoken words can be written, and that written words can be read. Michele will also use what he writes to help her assist him with word study, phonics, and phoneme development.

8 Christian correctly writes the five words without help (*I, go, to, the, two*). He correctly identifies many of the dominant sounds in the words.

9 The focus of the word study is to have Christian make words that rhyme with *hen*. This helps him understand that changing the beginning phoneme changes the word. It also helps him with letter and sound association.

10 These comments will be used to assist in planning small-group and one-on-one work during reader's workshop.

The data above and other data that Michele has collected on Christian across several weeks reveal that Christian has a strong command of African American Language (AAL) (see Chapter 6). He often abandons books that he believes are too difficult for him to read. When selecting books for his Browse Bags, he often counts the pages before choosing. If a book appears too long or he perceives it as challenging, he rarely adds it to his Browse Bag. He likes nonfiction about animals and fiction with adventurous characters.

While reading, Christian uses picture cues to problem-solve unknown words. Most of his approximations, or attempts at reading the unknown word, make sense and maintain the text's meaning, even when what he says does not match the word in the text. Take, for instance, the examples on the Daily Lesson Record. Christian said the word *rooster* for the word *hen*. This miscue made sense in the context of the text and did not detract from its overall meaning. Michele's focus for Christian to learn how to integrate cues when reading will assist him in becoming a proficient reader. Michele is also teaching Christian that spoken words can be written, and written words can be read. Word study, phonics, and phonemic awareness are not taught in isolation. Instead, Michele embeds word study, phonics, and phonemic awareness in the reading and writing that Christian does daily.

This data also reveals that when Christian reads something that does not make sense, he will reread it and self-correct until it does make sense. Other times, he rereads the text to confirm that what he read is correct. And there are times when his pronunciation and grammar are influenced by his command of AAL. Here is an example from the text *Little Chimp Is Brave*.

TEXT: Mother Chimp went up in the tree.

CHRISTIAN: Da muther went up da tree.

Without the knowledge that Christian was a speaker of AAL, Michele could have, at first glance, thought he did not comprehend the sentence. Teachers often mistakenly mark some student's use of AAL as miscues when the reading or pronunciation differs from what is in the text. Refer to Chapter 6 for more on this topic. Because Michele has worked with Christian since the beginning of school, she does not confuse his use of AAL with his comprehension of the text. She is cognizant that the overcorrection of a child makes it less likely that she or he will become a fluent reader (Perry & Delpit, 1998; Rasinski, 2006). His summary of the text only offers further evidence that he comprehends what he read. Based on these data, Michele places Christian and several other students in a flexible guided reading group to work on integrating cueing systems. Let's look at what transpires during this lesson.

THE ORAL READING RECORD

Michele captures Christian's oral reading by using miscue markings. She later analyzes his miscues to determine the cueing systems he relies on, an important part of her kidwatching assessment. We invite you to hone your skills by taking an oral reading record on several of your readers and analyzing their miscues to determine what patterns emerge. We believe this is an important step in learning about students' reading behaviors and linguistic features that are often neglected when time is limited. Below we have provided an alternative form that might be helpful to you as you work to notice the linguistic features students use as readers.

Word in Text	Student's Miscue	Semantic Does the miscue make sense?	Syntactic Is the miscue grammatically structured?	Grapho-phonemic Does the miscue look similar to the word in the text?	Self-Correction Did the child self-correct the miscue?	Home Language Is the child using his or her home language? What language and feature?

For a downloadable version of this form, go to scholastic.com/RevLoveResources.

Small-Group Instruction Through a Revolutionary Love Lens

Small-group instruction is another essential aspect of reader's workshop. Small-group instruction is often based on the assessment data collected during one-on-one conferences. You can form temporary guided reading groups to work with students who have similar needs as evidenced across your data. Small-group instruction can also be student-led with teacher guidance as students work in book clubs. Students should not be permanently placed in a certain small group and forced to remain there. Rather, small groups should be flexible and based on students' changing needs.

TEACHING READING BASED ON NEEDS

Teachers who embrace revolutionary love understand the importance of analyzing data, searching for patterns within and among data, interpreting the patterns, and planning instruction to meet the needs of their students. They don't group children based solely on their reading ability or level, but on their needs. As those needs change throughout the year, they regroup students. Teachers who embrace revolutionary love know what to look for, where to look, and how to quickly identify patterns when they present themselves. Equally important is their ability to engage children in instructional invitations that support them as meaning-makers. The patterns that emerged across Christian's data were as follows.

> Teachers who embrace revolutionary love know what to look for, where to look, and how to quickly identify patterns when they present themselves.

- He reads for meaning.
- He rereads to confirm.
- He self-corrects when his miscues do not make sense.
- He searches the picture to gain more cues to predict what the story is about or what an unknown word could possibly be.
- He summarizes what is read.
- At times his command of AAL influences his pronunciation and grammar when reading.
- Some of his miscues are not visually similar to the words in print (hen/rooster).

Michele works with Christian's small group for about 15 minutes to help them understand how to integrate or cross-check one cue with another to make a prediction and problem solve unknown words in the text. Michele selected *The Farm in Spring* because Christian is familiar with the topic of farm animals. The book also has a lot of picture support and poses just the right amount of challenge, which will help Christian build his confidence to effectively problem solve.

MICHELE: I noticed that when you came to this word [pointing to the word *hen*], you looked at the picture and then said the word *rooster*. What made you say *rooster*?

CHRISTIAN: I see a rooster in the picture.

MICHELE: That looks like one, doesn't it?

CHRISTIAN: Yes.

MICHELE: If you were to see the word *rooster* in this book, what letter would you expect to see at the beginning of the word?

CHRISTIAN: *R*.

MICHELE: Yes, so why can't this be *rooster*?

CHRISTIAN: No /r/.

MICHELE: You got it.

Michele has the group read the text. When students get to an unknown word, she encourages them to think about what would make sense, sound right, and look right in the sentence, requiring them to integrate their pragmatics or lived experiences with the semantic, graphophonemic, and syntactic cues. Michele will continue to focus on this strategy with these learners and collect kidwatching data to determine any new patterns that require instruction. Over time, Christian becomes more strategic and reads more books that present greater challenges. He eventually gets into graphic novels, but that takes intentional effort. The main goal here is for teachers to learn how to use their data to plan instruction and work with kids that pose challenges— eventually, with effort and motivation, moving into graphic novels. To support students like Christian, we continue to observe their language assets and patterns carefully and use our data to plan targeted, culturally attuned instruction that works for, rather than against, them.

CREATING CULTURALLY INCLUSIVE BOOK CLUBS

Discussions around texts should be at the heart of the reader's workshop. Book clubs are another way to engage students in discussions about texts and increase their understanding of them (Braden, 2019). Book clubs:

- help children learn from each other about ways to make sense of text.
- broaden and deepen children's understanding of texts in a variety of genres.
- guide children to understand that texts can be interpreted in multiple ways.
- support a positive classroom community by providing a safe venue for all children to share in small groups.
- create a dynamic in classrooms in which children function as discussion leaders.
- help students to work independently and contribute to the learning of others (Braden, 2019).

> "We can disagree and still love each other. Unless your disagreement is rooted in my oppression and denial of my humanity and right to exist."
>
> —**JAMES BALDWIN**

In Valente's fifth-grade classroom, Eliza and Valente' noticed the ways in which children spoke in depth about text that related to issues around injustices within society. After one student, Jaden, described how he and his father engaged in a discussion at home about activist and football player Colin Kaepernick, Eliza and Valente' decided to create a book club for families (Braden, Gibson, & Taylor-Gillette, 2020). This club became a safe space for families to talk as their children grew up observing the unjust practices to which Black and Latine people are subject. With the increasing number of instances of police brutality on Black and Latine bodies—including such cases as Sandra Bland, Trayvon Martin, Michael Brown, and Stephon Clark—they felt a need to create opportunities for families to talk about texts and issues that concerned them. On the following pages is a list of the books that Eliza and Valente' included in their unit.

Children's Literature on Social Injustice

***Brown Boy* by Daphnie Glenn** (2017)
Malik Wilson, a brilliant brown boy, is starting the third grade in a new school! Before he heads off to school, his mother gives him truths about being a brown boy today. Cities and neighborhoods where little brown boys and girls reside, have unfortunately been home to violence and senseless tragedies.

***Carter Reads the Newspaper* by Deborah Hopkinson** (2019)
Born to formerly enslaved parents, Carter G. Woodson pursued his love of reading and natural curiosity spending his life introducing others to the history of his people as the father of Black History Month.

***Grandpa, Is Everything Black Bad?* by Sandy Lynne Holman** (1998)
When Montsho, an African American boy, asks his grandfather "Is everything black bad?" his grandfather tells him about his African heritage and how his dark skin and his heritage are very good things.

Moves to Consider When Students Are Reading Books That Might Trigger Them

- Before beginning book clubs, build positive, affirming relationships with and among students (see Chapter 5).

- Continue with self-examination related to topics discussed in the books (see Chapter 2).

- Be open and vulnerable. Speak from your own experience and remember that everyone's experiences aren't the same.

- Let the children lead the discussion.

- When children say something that dishonors another's humanity, respond with questions that cause the child to explore how that statement may impact a friend or classmate. We often ask students, "Tell me more about that." For example, when a student used the *N*-word in Eliza's classroom, she asked the child to explain why he used the word:

    ELIZA: So, tell me more about why you use that word.

    STUDENT: My cousin says it all the time.

    ELIZA: What does it mean?

    STUDENT: He says it when someone makes him mad or he sees a Black person.

    ELIZA: So, he uses it to describe a person he does not like.

    STUDENT: Yes!

    ELIZA: How do you think that will make me feel or someone that matters to you who is Black?

    STUDENT: Oh!

    ELIZA: Yep. That would not feel good to me…what are you thinking right now?

    STUDENT: That if his Black friend heard him say that, that would be bad.

    ELIZA: Why?

    STUDENT: Because it would hurt his friend's feelings. We can't say things like that.

    ELIZA: Exactly. We don't want to say words that can make people of another race feel bad or hurt them. If we do, it means we judge them, or think less of them because of their race. Your cousin needs to change his words when he gets angry.

    STUDENT: I understand what you are saying. I'm going to tell him, and I'm not going to say that word either.

    ELIZA: This is something that we will continue to talk and think about as a class. We want to make sure that we honor others in our class and our lives with our words and actions.

- Allow your mistakes to serve as entry points for growing your knowledge.

I Am Alfonso Jones by **Tony Medina** (2017)

Alfonso Jones can't wait to play the role of Hamlet in his school's hip-hop rendition of the classic Shakespearean play. He also wants to let his best friend, Danetta, know how he really feels about her. But as he is buying his first suit, an off-duty police officer mistakes a clothes hanger for a gun, and he shoots Alfonso. Readers focus on police brutality and the Black Lives Matter movement.

Momma, Did You Hear the News? by **Sanya Whittaker Gragg** (2017)

Little Avery becomes concerned after seeing another police shooting of an unarmed man. His parents decide it is time to have "The Talk." They teach him and his brother a catchy chant to help remember what to do if approached by an officer, while also emphasizing that all policemen are not bad. A to the L to the I-V-E…come home ALIVE…. THAT is the key!

We Rise, We Resist, We Raise Our Voices by **Wade Hudson & Cheryl Willis Hudson** (2018)

What do we tell our children when the world seems bleak, and prejudice and racism run rampant? With 96 lavishly designed pages of original art and prose, 50 diverse creators lend voice to young activists.

In Summary

The reader's workshop is not a one-size-fits-all approach to teaching readers. Instead, teachers who embrace revolutionary love actively engage children in the work of reading texts they can and want to read. They engage the learner in the critical processing of text to make personal and community meaning of that text. And they build curricula that honors the diverse lived experiences that children bring with them to the classroom and use resources as windows, mirrors, and sliding glass doors (Bishop, 2007).

Chapter 9

LIBERATE WRITER'S WORKSHOP

Teachers who embrace revolutionary love believe that one reason writers write is to hold onto memories they cherish—moments that make them who they are. They write to discover what they know and have experienced. They write to release the pains and frustrations, and to express the joys and happiness of becoming their individual, unique selves. Teachers who embrace revolutionary love understand that the literacy curriculum they create with and for children should be designed to make spaces for children to live their lives out loud on the pages of their journals or notebooks. Writer's workshop as a revolutionary loving practice invites children to tell the stories of their lives in a supportive and affirming space, allowing students to develop as writers. We also get to know students when we ask them to share their oral stories, drawings, and writing that are a daily part of writer's workshop. Many scholars who center children of color describe writing and its purposes as a key literacy practice for those students to make meaning of their identities (Muhammad, 2020). Additionally, when given the opportunity to engage in authentic writing experiences, students can draw on a wealth of resources, including the experiences of other students, to write about their lives (Rodriguez, 2017).

In this chapter, we provide an overview of the writer's workshop as practiced with a revolutionary love stance. We discuss common writing practices that educators typically use during the workshop and give you opportunities to reflect on your own practices. From there, we take a sneak peek into Jacqui Witherspoon's classroom as she engages her students in a unit focused on hair and hair styles. We explore ways to create writing assessments with your students that draw on their brilliance and skills. We close the chapter with an explanation of how the actions of teachers who embrace principles of revolutionary love support Black and Latine writers and how you can emulate such practices.

An Overview of Writer's Workshop

Teachers who embrace revolutionary love know that writer's workshop invites students to tell stories about their lives. It is an opportunity to get to know students by inviting their voices in the classroom through the sharing of oral stories, drawings, or writing. Many of you may be familiar with the structure of the writer's workshop. As a framework for teaching writing, writer's workshop should afford students opportunities to write daily (Graves, 1983; Ray, 1999). The components of a writer's workshop include a mini-lesson, writing time while the teacher confers with individual students, and a time to share.

- **Mini-Lesson/Mentor Texts:** The teacher engages the students in explicit demonstrations that are designed to promote writer's crafts and/or skill development.
- **Independent Writing:** Students work independently for an extended time daily on their writing by planning, drafting, revising, rereading, and editing.
- **Conferring:** The teacher meets daily with individual students and provides feedback on their writing. She takes anecdotal notes and uses those notes to later plan a curriculum that best supports the needs of her writers.
- **Share Time:** Students have opportunities to share their writing with partners, small groups, or the whole class.

A teacher who embraces revolutionary love understands that writer's workshop is an opportunity to teach students how to write in connection with their experiences and values, and that their stories are worth writing about, that they belong, and that they are safe sharing those stories. We offer a detailed look into a writer's workshop that honors the lives, stories, and literacies of Black and Latine students. We begin with the oral tradition of storytelling and the importance of developing a community of writers within the context of students' experiences and identities.

COMMON WRITING PRACTICES

If you ask teachers what's most important when it comes to writing instruction, you will undoubtedly get a varied response. Some may say teaching the writing process is most important. Others may say it's the traits of writing. Some teachers prioritize the five-paragraph essay, while others focus on prompts that mirror on-demand writing for standardized writing assessments. Some teachers provide scaffolds, templates, graphic organizers, and acronyms (e.g., RAFT, ACE) to support students' writing. Often, we align our instruction with a finished writing product. As you read this chapter, we want you to reflect on your beliefs and pay close attention to the shifts in practices that you make or consider.

Time and again research has shown that writing instruction is more focused on children's writing products than their writing process. Lee-Heart (2018) explains that writing is subjective, intimate, and contextual, yet Black and Latine children often experience writing instruction as being forced into a box many sizes too small. Writing practices that are often employed in schools with predominantly Black and Latine children tend to include worksheets, spelling or dictation activities, and/or writing to a given prompt. These practices focus more on the writing product than on the writers themselves. In working with educators in a variety of roles (literacy instructor, literacy consultant or coach), we have found that in schools with predominantly Black and Latine populations, authentic methods such as writer's workshop are less often implemented. Let's take a moment to reflect on common writing practices and how writing instruction grounded in revolutionary love is essential in developing writers and not just the finished writing product.

Common Writing Practices	Problem With Practice	Revolutionary Practice
Goal: Support emergent/ younger writers **Instructional Practice:** Prompted writing: "I like…", "I can…"	• While it is important for students to learn how to write sentences, the writer's workshop should allow students' writing to follow their oral language. • Hinders idea development	• Create anchor charts based on students' experiences in the community and using them as resources in writing. • Create personal charts for children that include pictures of their family and places that are important to them. • Teach a mini-lesson for students about labeling and writing what they say.
Goal: High-Volume Academic Writing **Instructional Practice:** Formulaic Writing (five-paragraph essay, Beginning-Middle-End narrative structure)	• Hinders creativity • Lacks relevance and meaning • Limits students' voices and agency in their writing • Sometimes these kinds of papers are just boring.	• Encourage writing about students' lives and experiences. • Allow students' lives to be a part of the writing in the classroom.
Goal: Focus on grammar and conventions **Instructional Practice:** Dictation and grammar worksheets	• Disregards students' linguistic resources that are not mainstream English • Skills are often taught in isolation and rarely applied to students' own writing.	• Encourage writing that focuses on communicating ideas clearly. Students edit their own writing or work with a peer to edit, but the focus on grammar and conventions is not the focus of the teaching and assessment.
Goal: Help students write to be prepared for standardized test **Instructional Practice:** Only writing to specific prompts provided by the teacher	• Prompts are not typically relevant to students, and sometimes students have limited knowledge of the prompt. • Limits students' idea development and creativity • Shapes students' beliefs that writing is constrained to this format	• Have students write about topics that matter to them. In this way, students have an authentic investment in the writing. Students can write from the heart and make sense of their worlds.

REFLECTING ON WRITING PRACTICES

Take a moment to reflect in your notebook about your instructional writing practices. Do they support students with meaning-making in connection with their identities? Do they draw on students' lived experiences? As you read about the writer's workshop grounded in revolutionary love, what shifts can you make immediately to support your writers and awaken their identities and voices?

GETTING TO KNOW STUDENTS AS WRITERS

Knowing your students as writers helps you to personalize the writer's workshop as you build on students' strengths and plan curriculum to grow them as writers.

Writing Interest Survey 2.0

As an alternative to a traditional Writing Interest Survey on the following page, we offer this "2.0" version. Use the Writing Interest Survey 2.0 to help you understand facets of your students as writers, and how they engage in the writing process.

Writing Interest Survey 2.0

Name:

1. Do you like writing? Why or why not?

2. What do you write about?

3. What do you like writing about?

4. What don't you like writing about?

5. How do you capture moments that you want to remember?

6. What support do you need to become a better writer?

7. Name a piece of writing that you enjoyed listening to when read aloud (e.g., book, poem, nonfiction story, song lyrics).

8. What authors do you like?

9. What is the best story you've ever written?

Family Member/ Guardian

1. What type of writing do you do at home with your family members?

2. How is important information captured in your family?

EXAMINING YOUR BELIEFS ABOUT WRITING AND WRITERS

Before we delve into the details of writer's workshop, we want you to take a moment to reflect on your current beliefs about the writers in your classroom and the teaching of writing. In your notebook, respond to the following questions.

- What do you believe is the purpose for teaching writing? What do you envision for your students as writers?
- How do you define the writing process?
- What is essential for you as an educator to know and be able to do when supporting writers?
- How do you structure your writing time? Do you incorporate writer's workshop? If so, what is essential? If not, what do you do to support students during writing instruction?
- How often are students allowed to write in your room?

CREATING A COMMUNITY OF WRITERS

To avoid the problematic practices that are often evidenced in many classrooms serving Black and Latine students, we want to offer you structures that support your students as empowered writers who write about what matters to them. We begin with oral storytelling. Oral tradition (see Chapter 4) in a writer's workshop challenges the stringent way we think of writing in schools and provides a foundation that supports all students to view themselves as writers. Oral history or storytelling is indeed a component of writing. Oral storytelling in the writer's workshop disrupts the dominant cultural norm (Okun, 1998) that the written word is highly valued over any other form of knowledge sharing, although many communities of color have a rich history of oral tradition. The oral stories that children tell become the stories that they will draw and write about during the year. One of the ways that you can begin the year in a writer's workshop is by creating space for students to tell their everyday stories. This is a great way to get to know the students and their funds of knowledge (Moll, Amanti, Neff, & Gonzales, 1992). Here are some steps to take to begin oral storytelling:

1. **Begin by letting the class know that they will be telling stories just like Jacqueline Woodson (or any other authors you have read in class).** Be sure to share with students the diverse storytelling traditions of Black and Latine authors

and poets. Devise a system so that each student gets a chance to tell a personal story to the class. Invite students to sit close to the speaker so that they can hear each story.

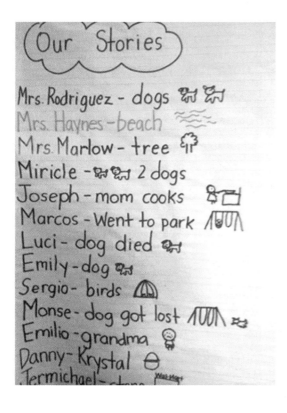

2. **Create a large chart titled "Our Stories" and begin by telling your own story.** It's important for your students to view you as a writer and storyteller. Think of everyday stories that you can share with your students. Make sure they get the message that their everyday stories about going to the store or going to the park are worth sharing. Don't set the stage by telling a story about going to a big theme park; students will want to tell a story just as exciting as that, even if they have never had that experience. Allow students to share their stories in the language that they are most comfortable using.

3. **Capture the stories on the "Our Stories" chart for everyone to see.** You may want to include a picture if you are working with kindergartners or first graders. Provide an opportunity for everyone in the class to tell a story that is important to them. Note that this may take several days.

4. **Show how you can take an oral story and make it into a written story by modeling with your personal story during a whole-group mini-lesson.** Go back to the chart that you have made with students as you were telling the story. Retell the oral story by looking at the notes and quick picture that was drawn. Part of the work may be to help the students think about what will be written down based on the oral story that has been told. Be mindful that all stories do not have to be written. They can be recorded or simply told to provide practice in storytelling. Here's an example of how a teacher moved from the oral storytelling to the writing:

Ms. Rodriguez: *Writers, remember that we have been telling stories about our lives. We have also read stories by famous authors that have told their own stories like Jacqueline Woodson and Yuyi Morales. I told a story about how I took my dogs for a walk and my dog Mimi got away. I can look at this picture on the chart and think about the story that I shared with you. Now my work is to think about what words I will write down to tell my story. I want to begin by drawing my picture to make sure that it matches my words. After that, I want to write the words from my story. I am going to write: I went for a walk with my dogs. My dog Mimi pulled on her leash and ran away from me.*

Using oral storytelling to begin the writer's workshop not only allows students to share their lives with the class and with others, but it also allows students to engage in listening to their peers and learning about the lives and experiences of others. This helps to develop the cultural competence of students and allows them to view the world through a lens other than their own.

Example of a Writer's Workshop That Begins With Oral Storytelling

We invite you into the classroom of a teacher who Eliza often works with. Jacqui embodies revolutionary love. She plans daily opportunities for students to engage in the writing process and create stories about things that matter to them. Jacqui begins her daily, hour-long writer's workshop with a whole-group mini-lesson that focuses on a skill she wants her writers to employ in their own writing.

The mini-lessons are followed by a 40-minute independent writing time. During this time, students talk to one another about their writing, refer to books that they have read, or write on their own. Jacqui uses this time to confer with her writers. Her goal is to confer with each of her students at least once a week. The writer's workshop concludes with students sharing their writing.

At first, Jacqui followed a prescribed writing curriculum that did not align with her students' cultural backgrounds or interests. The unit was focused on writing a personal narrative with a focus on "small moments" and writing details. The books that were suggested in the mini-lessons featured mostly White characters and included experiences that were not familiar to her students. Jacqui decided that she would redesign the unit to better fit the needs of her students. Instead of using the recommended texts, she selected culturally relevant mentor texts and decided to focus on "hair moments." Although Jacqui changed the topics she talked about, she continued to have high expectations for her students, and she met the standards required by the mandated curriculum.

This "hair moments" unit came about when one morning students started talking about the different ways she wore her hair. They began to create a list of hairstyles that she wore and that the students wore.

JACQUI: We have a list with lots of hairstyles. What are some of the hairstyles that you have worn on the list?

STUDENT 1: I wear ponytails and braids.

STUDENT 2: I wear cornrows.

JACQUI: I have worn cornrows before, too. They were braided so tight that I had a headache all night, but I thought they were so cute! My mom braided them for me. I just had a thought. You all know we've been reading books about small moments and the ways that we can zoom into a moment when we are writing.

STUDENTS: Yes!

JACQUI: Would you all like to write about your hair moments when we write our small moments?

STUDENTS: Yes!

JACQUI: Okay, we can start by sharing stories about memorable experiences we've had with hairstyles. Just like I did about my cornrows. We have a few minutes for just about two students right now, then we will tell more stories this afternoon. Who would like to share?

STUDENT 3: One time me and my cousins went to get our hair braided. We got beads on our hair, and they made noise when we shook our hair.

JACQUI: You had noisy braids! That's going to make a good story to write. I can't wait to read all the details. Who else?

STUDENT 4: The barber put my initials in my hair one time. It looked so good! It was fresh! I want to get it again.

JACQUI: Your barber is really good, then. I can't wait to hear more stories. Telling your stories about your hair will help you when we start writing our small moments.

This conversation about hairstyles led to storytelling around hair moments. These stories guided Jacqui with the types of texts she used for mini-lessons and provided a foundation for students to develop as writers by centering their lived experiences.

MINI-LESSONS

Mini-lessons are short, focused lessons that support students with understanding features/ characteristics of writing. It's an opportunity to model strategies to help students develop and improve their writing and to tap into the joy and creativity of being a writer. During mini-lessons, we explicitly model our thinking processes aloud as we brainstorm, draft, and review our own writing pieces as examples for students. We also use mentor texts to teach a skill we'd like students to practice in their writing. When the writer's workshop is grounded in revolutionary love, teachers are intentional when selecting mentor texts that reflect their students' lives. Students need to see themselves reflected in the mentor texts and to see beyond themselves to understand others whose experiences are different from their own. Below, we provide examples of mini-lessons from Ms. Witherspoon's unit on "Hair Moments."

Eliza, Caitlyn, Jacqui, and Valente' at the Equity in Education Conference hosted by the Center of Excellence for the Education and Equity of African American Students

Mini-lesson 1: Writers create a list of memorable small moments.

Mentor Text: *Crown: An Ode to the Fresh Cut* by Derrick Barnes

1. Read *Crown: An Ode to the Fresh Cut* to students.

2. Brainstorm a list of hairstyles with students, for example:

   - Braids
   - Short Cut
   - Beads
   - Braided Crown
   - Relaxer/Perm

3. Using Class Dojo, Remind, or another messaging tool, ask parents to send in photos of their kids with different or new hairstyles or ask students to interview parents on hair moments.

Mini-lesson 2: Writers share and partner-write their small moments.

1. Share a hair story, or "hair moment," with the class.

2. Have students take two to three minutes to share their own "hair moments" with a friend. You may notice as kids share that they are confusing big moments with small moments, and that's fine. You will need to step in with an organizer to help them find their small moments. See examples below.

3. Ask them to return to their seats to do a *quick-write*.

4. Define *quick-write* for students.

Small Moment Organizers

Snow Moments	
Big Topic	One day it snowed outside.
Smaller Topic	I went outside to play in the snow.
Small Topic	I had a snowball fight with my friends.

Hair Moments	
Big Topic	"I went to a salon with my sister."
Smaller Topic	"I went to the salon to get my hair braided."
Small Topic	"I got my hair braided in cornrows, and my sister got box braids."

Mini-lesson 3: Writers make a mental movie of what happened, using details.

Choose one of these options:

- Use your hair moment as a frame.

- Return to your anchor text to study the way the author tells his or her story, bit by bit:

    Writers, today I would like for you to share every detail of your small moment that we found yesterday. Let's look back at the way Mr. Barnes shares the main characters' experiences in detail.

Family Connection: If time permits, you might work with a parent to come in to tell their child's hair moment or ask him or her to share images or audio (using Voice Memo or Class Dojo, etc.).

Mini-lesson 4: Writers crack open their sentences by adding details.

Use the chart at right to model how to add details to a piece of writing. Then have students try it with their own writing.

Image	Sounds
Close your eyes: What is in front of you? Who is there? What is there?	*What do you hear? Who do you hear?*
Feelings	**Light**
As you picture your image, what do you feel in that moment?	*Describe the colors: Is it dull/light/bright?*
Smells	**Other Questions?**
What do you smell?	

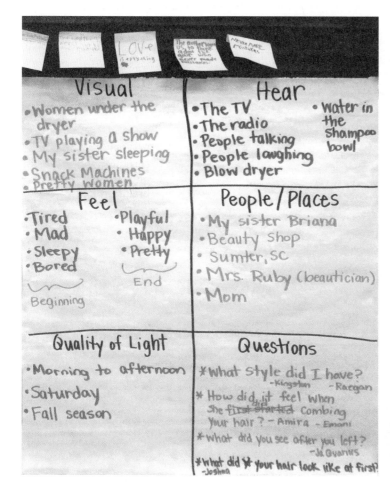

Sensory Details Anchor Chart created by Jacqui and her students using Georgia Heard's "Six Room Poem"

MENTOR TEXTS

When choosing mentor texts, remember to include titles that *all* children can connect with. See the lists below for mentor text ideas. We've included the books that Ms. Witherspoon intentionally selected to address the experiences of her students for the "Hair Moments" unit, as well as mentor texts related to name stories (see Chapter 2 for a detailed description of name stories), and other culturally diverse texts suited to specific forms of writing. Although the following lists include book selections, keep in mind that mentor texts can include less traditional options, such as songs, poems, or pictures.

Mentor Texts for Hair Moments

Bippy Bop Barbershop **by Natasha Anastasia Tarpley**
Miles goes to the barber shop with his dad for the first time. This book highlights the bonds between boys and men in barbershops, and the special moment of getting a first haircut.

Emi's Curly, Coily, Cotton Candy Hair
by Tina Olajide
Emi is a little girl with a BIG imagination. In this story, she sends a positive message about her BIG, curly, coily hair.

Furqan's First Flat Top/El Primer Corte de Mesita de Furqan **by Robert Liu-Trujillo**
Furqan, a 10-year-old Black Latino boy, has always had curly hair and decides to have his hair cut for the first time. His dad suggests a flat-top fade, but at the barbershop Furqan worries that his haircut will look funny. Before he realizes it, though, the barber has finished his cut, and Furqan realizes his first flat top is the freshest!

Hair Love by Matthew A. Cherry

Based on Matthew A. Cherry's award-winning animated short of the same name, *Hair Love* celebrates the relationship between a father and daughter while also celebrating Black hair. Zuri's mom has been away, and she wants an extra special hairstyle to welcome her home.

Hair Story by NoNieqa Ramos

In this book, two girls—one Black and one non-Black Puerto Rican—play hair salon. Inspired by the past, family members, and cultural icons, they discover the stories their hair can tell.

Hairs/Pelitos by Sandra Cisneros

This story in English and Spanish describes a family in which each member has a different hair type.

I Love My Hair! by Natasha Anastasia Tarpley

Every night, Keyana sits down between her mother's knees to have her hair combed. Although her mom is gentle, it still hurts Keyana sometimes. Her mom reminds her of how lucky she is to wear her Black hair in so many beautiful styles. This story celebrates the importance of having pride in your hair.

Mentor Texts for Name Stories

Alma and How She Got Her Name
by Juana Martinez-Neal

Alma's father shares the story of how Alma got her name from family members. In the process, Alma realizes that her name is special.

My Name Is an Address by Ekuwah Mends Moses

What's in a name? Ekuwah Mends Moses answers that question using the alphabet letters in her name. She learns about her family, history, culture, language, and geography when she researches her name.

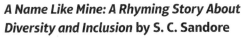

A Name Like Mine: A Rhyming Story About Diversity and Inclusion by S. C. Sandore

A rhythmic book that reminds readers of the importance of showing respect by pronouncing people's names correctly.

Your Name Is a Song by Jamilah Thompkins-Bigelow

A little girl experiences her first day of school with everyone mispronouncing her name. Her mother tells her to tell her teacher that her name is a song. So she does. She returns to school and teaches everyone that your name can be a song.

Mentor Texts for Teaching Narrative Writing

Carmela Full of Wishes by Matt de la Peña

Carmela wakes up on her birthday and is finally old enough to join her big brother on the family errands. She finds a dandelion growing in the pavement, and her brother tells her she must make a wish before she blows the white fluff. What wish will Carmela make?

Mentor Text Idea: Embedding the setting throughout the text, using descriptive language, and varying sentences

Jabari Jumps by Gaia Cornwall

After Jabari completes his swimming lessons, he's ready to jump off the diving board... or so he thinks!

Mentor Text Idea: Stretching a small moment over several pages

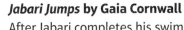

***A Moon for Moe and Mo* by Jane Breskin Zalben**
Moses Feldman, a Jewish boy, lives at one end of Flatbush Avenue in Brooklyn, New York, while Mohammed Hassan, a Muslim boy, lives at the other. One day they meet at a market and are mistaken for brothers, and a friendship is born.

Mentor Text Idea: Developing a setting and characters; writing a beginning, middle, and end; and identifying a problem and solution of the story

Mentor Texts for Teaching Opinion Writing

The Little Book of Little Activists
by Penguin Young Readers
This book is an inspiring photo essay that includes examples of kids' opinions about real-life causes.

Mentor Text Idea: Connecting opinion writing to activism

***One Word from Sophia* by Jim Averbeck**
Sophia has one true desire for her birthday. But she has to convince her mom, dad, Uncle Conrad, and Grand-mama. Will she be able to?

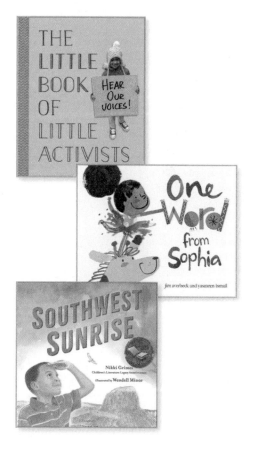

Mentor Text Idea: Considering audience and word choice in opinion writing

***Southwest Sunrise* by Nikki Grimes**
A young boy moves from New York to New Mexico, and when he first arrives to his new home, he hates it. As the story continues, he explores all New Mexico has to offer, and his opinion begins to change.

Mentor Text Idea: Developing reasons and support for opinions

Mentor Texts for Teaching Biography

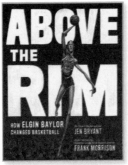

Above the Rim: How Elgin Baylor Changed Basketball by **Jen Bryant**

Basketball Hall-of-Famer Elgin Baylor was one of the game's all-time-greatest players, who inspired others on and off the court. But when traveling for away games, many hotels and restaurants turned Elgin away because he was Black. One night, Elgin had enough and staged a one-man protest that captured the attention of the press, the public, and the NBA.

Mentor Text Idea: Using figurative language in biographies

Dream Builder: The Story of Architect Philip Freelon by **Kelly Starling Lyons**

This book chronicles the life of acclaimed architect, Philip Freelon, from high school, to college at Hampton University (a historically Black institution), to the point in his career when he entered a competition with two fellow architects to design the National Museum of African American History and Culture.

Mentor Text Idea: Using metaphors in biographies

Nelson Mandela: No Easy Walk to Freedom by **Barry Denenberg**

This powerful biography provides an in-depth look at Nelson Mandela, who grew up in a rural village in South Africa under racist apartheid rule—a regime he ultimately helped overthrow. Denenberg explores the history of South Africa and its often violent struggle for civil rights, while tracing Mandela's role in that history.

Nina: A Story of Nina Simone by **Traci N. Todd**

Born Eunice Kathleen Waymon in small-town North Carolina, Nina Simone was a musical child. She sang before she talked and learned to play piano at a very young age. During her first performances under the name of Nina Simone, her voice was rich and sweet, but as the Civil Rights Movement gained steam, Nina's voice soon became a thunderous roar as she raised her voice in powerful protest in the fight against racial inequality and discrimination.

Planting Stories: The Life of Librarian and Storyteller Pura Belpré by Anika Aldamuy Denise

When she came to America in 1921, Pura Belpré carried the cuentos folklóricos of her Puerto Rican homeland. Finding a new home at the New York Public Library as a bilingual assistant, she turned her popular retellings into libros and spread story seeds across the land.

Mentor Text Idea: Identifying features of biographies, such as important dates, areas of achievement, and the impact the subject has on his or her field

Schomburg: The Man Who Built a Library by Carole Boston Weatherford

Amid the scholars, poets, authors, and artists of the Harlem Renaissance stood an Afro–Puerto Rican named Arturo Schomburg. This law clerk's life's passion was to collect books, letters, music, and art from Africa and the African diaspora and bring to light the achievements of people of African descent through the ages. A century later, his groundbreaking collection, known as the Schomburg Center for Research in Black Culture, has become a beacon to scholars all over the world.

Soldier for Equality: José de la Luz Sáenz and the Great War by Duncan Tonatiuh

José de la Luz Sáenz, or Luz, was born in the United States but experienced prejudice because of his Mexican heritage. He joined the army to fight in World War I and became part of the Intelligence Office in Europe, but he was not recognized for his contributions. Experiences like those led him to fight for equality for Mexicans and to start the League of United Latin American Citizens (LULAC).

Mentor Text Idea: Focusing on a particular time or event in someone's life, instead of her or his whole life

Sonia Sotomayor: A Judge Grows in the Bronx by Jonah Winter

Before Supreme Court Justice Sonia Sotomayor took her seat in our nation's highest court, she was just a little girl in the South Bronx. Justice Sotomayor didn't have a lot growing up, but she had what she needed—her mother's love, a will to learn, and her own determination. With bravery, she became the person she wanted to be.

Conferring: Providing Feedback Through a Revolutionary Love Lens

An important part of writer's workshop is conferring. While writers are engaged in independent writing, educators can rotate around the room and confer one on one with students to guide their writing development. Some educators may approach conferences as an opportunity to look at students' writing for errors that need to be fixed. But those who embrace revolutionary love understand that individual writing and conferring time should focus on strategy instruction to help the writer. These educators confer to learn about who their students are as writers and to recognize and support their writing strengths and gifts. Uncovering a writer's strengths is made possible when we know and value the diverse, cultural writing resources that students bring into the classroom. As you talk to your writers about their writing, it is important to respond first as a human and then as an educator. Writers are sharing stories from their lives, and we must honor their work.

> Uncovering a writer's strengths is made possible when we know and value the diverse, cultural writing resources that students bring into the classroom.

Let's revisit Ms. Witherspoon's class as she confers with Ahmed. On Day 3 of the hair unit, students were taught to make a mental movie of what happened and to tell their story bit by bit in small details. As Ms. Witherspoon conferred with Ahmed, she asked him to read his piece aloud. As she listened, she captured kidwatching notes. She noticed that Ahmed wrote a funny story about the time the barber combed out his hair that had grown out, when he had an afro. She also noticed that Ahmed used big, descriptive words at the beginning of his writing to explain bit by bit what happened and to describe how he felt about his big hair. For the remainder of the story, he veered away from detailed writing and instead wrote about the episode as a "big topic." Ms. Witherspoon made sure to focus on Ahmed's strength as a detailed writer. She pointed out how the first part of the story helped her to see the episode as a movie in her mind's eye. She also noted that the second part of the story did not have as many details, which made it hard for her to experience those moments bit by bit. She then asked Ahmed how he could apply his gift for creating a vivid scene through details to the second half of the story so it would be as lively as the first part.

	Writer's Workshop Conference Form		
Student name: *Caleb*			
Date	**Information About the Writing**	**What Is the Student Doing Well?**	**Teaching Point**
3/1	*Writing a personal narrative about going to Mexico with his family.*	*• Has included personal details about the story* *• Includes some dialogue*	*Including a topic sentence and following with details that matter about the trip*
3/7	*Working on final draft of narrative story about going to Mexico; Proofreading*	*• The piece includes topic sentences followed by details about the trip.* *• Able to hear his voice*	*Punctuation— Reading the piece aloud to make sure that the correct punctuation is added*
3/14	*Starting a new piece; researching info for an informational piece focused on ocean pollution*	*• Chose a topic that he cares about* *• Researching the topic and writing facts that he is finding about the topic*	*Organizing the information helped him think about how to search for information/take notes*

In this conference form, there is ample space to record a student's strengths—an important component of the process. For a downloadable version, go to scholastic.com/RevLoveResources.

Sharing Work Through a Revolutionary Love Lens

An important part of writer's workshop is sharing time, when students "go public" with their writing. Sharing time is the perfect opportunity for students to become experts and share their knowledge with their peers. We believe that students should be affirmed as writing experts and recognized for the genius they bring to their writing. When we approach sharing time through a revolutionary love lens, we make sure to showcase both finished works and works in progress. If we only call on students with finished work to share, we unintentionally send the message that writing is about the product. It is just as important, if not more so, to showcase students with works in progress. Remember, we want to teach the whole writer, not the one piece of writing. With that goal in mind, here are some questions to use as you guide your writers during the share time:

- What do you think you did well as a writer?
- What did you learn as you were writing this piece?
- What can your writing teach us?
- What is something new you tried in your writing?
- What did you try from the mentor text?

Questions such as these elicit thoughtful responses and create engaging discussions.

At the beginning of the year, the moderating may fall largely to the teacher, but the goal should be for students to lead the conversations about their writing and to learn from each other.

Writing Assessment Through a Revolutionary Love Lens

Writing assessments provide opportunities to learn about students' writing strengths, highlight students' growth, and gather information to guide further instruction. In traditional writer's workshops, a rubric is commonly used to assess whether a student's writing is below level, on level, or exceeds the grade-level writing standards. Yet, any "standard" that is embedded in education is based on Eurocentric norms and values. When we assess with revolutionary love, we identify the strengths that writers possess and understand the cultural resources that writers use in their writing that are not always indicated in standardized rubrics. For example, sometimes bilingual students incorporate words from their home language because they may have more command in that language and are better able to articulate their thoughts. This is a strength that is not captured in standard rubrics but that demonstrates a student's ability to draw on their linguistic resources in their writing.

NOTICING STRENGTHS

1. Look at the writing sample below.

2. What are the student's strengths?

3. What do you notice that could inform your teaching and build on the student's strengths and cultural resources?

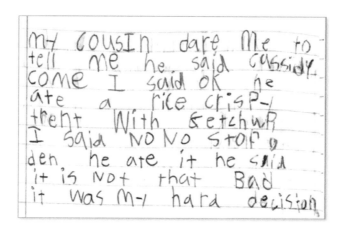

HOLISTIC RUBRICS

Students will find more meaning, relevance, and joy in school-based writing if they have a role in the creation of criteria and assignments. In the excerpt below, Natasha is talking with a small group of first graders who elected to write a skit for a unit on kindness. As they begin writing their scripts, Natasha has a conversation with the students about what they think would make a really good script. That is the first step she takes with them to co-create a writing rubric.

NATASHA: I'm excited to learn from you all about how you want to create your skits. We have already discussed parts of the skit, like the opening and how you want to share facts about the importance of being kind. Now, how will you know if you wrote your skit well?

MICAH: My skit is about kindness…

ISAIAH: Ways to show kindness!

NATASHA: Okay, this is what I'm hearing, to show what you have learned from all the books you've read, your skit must be about kindness?

RILEY: Yes!

ISAIAH: We want you to be kind and show other people to be kind.

MICAH: It's a message, I mean... no... a skit about kindness.

NATASHA: OK! Having a message in a skit is important, because a message can help people think about being what.....

MICAH &
ISAIAH: Kind!

ISAIAH: A good message that help people. That inspire people.

NATASHA: Inspire people.... When you say inspire what do you mean?

ISAIAH: It inspires people to be kind.

NATASHA: So, a good skit would help people remember to be kind?

ISAIAH: Yes.

NATASHA: OK, so the topic must be about kindness and the message must be strong to inspire people. What will help us know when a message is strong or inspires people? Should we have facts about kindness?

MICAH &
ISAIAH: Yes!

RILEY: Why you gotta be kind.

NATASHA: What else makes a message strong?

ISAIAH: It inspires people.

NATASHA: It inspires people. What can be added to the facts that tell people why you must be kind?

ISAIAH: Like show, show people, like when Titus was kind to me when I didn't have my book, he gave me his.

NATASHA: That was kind of him. So, include facts and give an example of kindness?

ISAIAH: Yes!

NATASHA: Okay, this is what we will work on when writing our skit. Great job!

During the conversation Natasha took notes and created a rubric with one column for the criteria the students named: *Good message that inspires people to be kind*; *Opening matches the topic of kindness*; *At least two facts about kindness*; and *At least one example of kindness*. The idea of creating a holistic rubric with only one column for criteria maintains the expectation that this is what all the students will be able to demonstrate this skill at some point. It emphasizes the belief that all students are strong writers who are able to demonstrate the skill as well as continued areas that the students can grow in.

Writing Rubric

Student name: *Caleb*

Criteria	Examples of Demonstrated Skill	Opportunities for Growth
Good message that inspires people to be kind	*Your script gives reasons why being kind is a good thing to do. That is inspiring.*	*Think about your audience and ask yourself whether your message is getting across.*
Opening matches the topic of kindness	*Your opening was funny! I laughed out loud! This will capture the audience's attention.*	*The opening did not mention kindness. Remember to stay on topic throughout.*
At least two facts about kindness	*You have three facts about kindness. Great job!*	
At least one example of kindness	*Your example supported your facts and was a great a way to show why being kind is important. Your writing helped me to visualize what was happening!*	

For a downloadable version of this rubric, go to scholastic.com/RevLoveResources.

1. Talk to the students about the purpose of the writing and the audience. List their thoughts.

2. Ask the students to recall mini-lessons they have been taught in the writer's workshop. What did they learn that they want to include in this writing? List these ideas, too.

3. Ask the students what else is needed to make the writing feel like their own. How can they represent their identities and interests in their writing?

It is important to view writing assessment as an opportunity to learn about the students' writing strengths and highlight students' growth, and use that information to guide further instruction.

Writing Celebrations

One of the most important things that you can do as a teacher is allow students to feel successful and to celebrate them as writers. Writing celebrations are opportunities to showcase students' writing and to include families. As a teacher, you can set a date for the writing celebration and ask students to work toward having a published piece of writing that they can share. Here are some steps to take to prepare for a writing celebration.

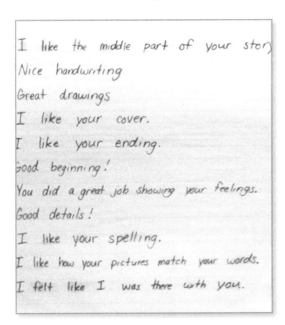

I like the middle part of your story
Nice handwriting
Great drawings
I like your cover.
I like your ending.
Good beginning!
You did a great job showing your feelings.
Good details!
I like your spelling.
I like how your pictures match your words.
I felt like I was there with you.

1. Let students know about the writing celebration date. It's important for students to be able to work toward having a published piece by a certain date.

2. Help students consider what it means to have a published piece of writing (including a cover and an "about the author" page, and making sure that the writing is readable).

3. Invite family members or other classes to the writing celebration.

4. Make a list of questions to ask other writers as students read each other's work.

Anchor chart with things that students say to other writers during a writing celebration

5. Allow students and family members an opportunity to read students' work. Provide sticky notes so that visitors and students can write notes to the students.

The educators we highlighted in this chapter were intentional as they created powerful spaces for writers to engage in the writing process. These educators were also intentional and reflective about planning and providing opportunities for writers to learn from other authors, through the mini-lessons they witnessed, and through the feedback from their classmates and teacher. Now that we have shared with you how teachers who embrace revolutionary loving practices create a writer's workshop that centers the writers as they engage in the process of writing, we invite you to consider the thought processes that are necessary to do this work well. As you plan your next writer's workshop, here are some questions and tasks to consider.

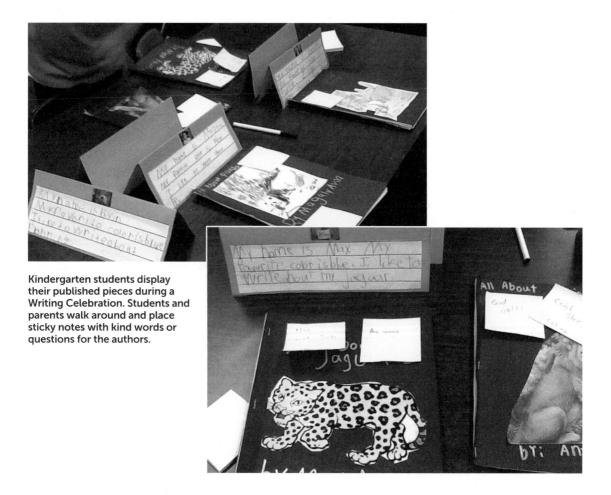

Kindergarten students display their published pieces during a Writing Celebration. Students and parents walk around and place sticky notes with kind words or questions for the authors.

Writer's Workshop Component	Questions to Guide Planning	Tasks
Mini-Lesson/ Mentor Texts	• What crafting techniques do students need to know to improve their writing? • What strategy can support them with developing the craft? • What texts provide a mirror for students' lives and are an example of the writing craft/genre/skill? • What texts include students' cultural and linguistic resources that support writing development?	• Select mentor texts that make connections to students and that connect to crafting techniques • Plan mini-lessons that provide an explicit demonstration of the crafting technique. • Select a variety of texts that are windows, mirrors, and sliding glass doors to use during the writer's workshop.
Independent Writing/ Conferring	• What are the goals of the writing unit? • Do the goals align with the students' strengths and cultural resources as writers? • What specific teaching points are needed to support the students with meeting the writing goals? • How can the students' writing strengths be affirmed during writing conferences?	• Notice what the students do well when writing, even if it's not a feature of the writing focus. • Provide the student a teaching point that supports students with meeting the writing goal and developing as a writer while affirming students' writing strengths
Share Time	• What procedure do you need to put in place to ensure that all students have opportunities to share excerpts of their writing? • What strategies do you have in place to affirm what your writers have done? • What strategies do you have in place to provide supportive feedback to grow your writers?	• Make sure that you have a way to track which writers have shared across the week.

In Summary

Teachers who embrace revolutionary love center their students' lives and voices in the curriculum in supportive and affirming ways. When students' lives and voices are at the center of our writer's workshop, we validate their everyday experiences and celebrate them as writers. We provide opportunities for writers to engage in authentic writing experiences, to draw on a wealth of resources, including other students' knowledge, and to share their expertise as writers. Students enter the literacy classrooms as bold, brilliant writers, and it's only through revolutionary love that we can allow their rich, cultural identities to guide their development as writers.

CLOSING REFLECTION When you lead with love—revolutionary love— incredible possibilities for connection open up. Our hope is that, by reading this book, you will embrace the principles of revolutionary love and spread it in your classroom, school, and beyond.

CHILDREN'S BOOKS CITED

Above the Rim: How Elgin Baylor Changed Basketball by Jen Bryant (Harry N. Abrams, 2020)

Africa, Amazing Africa: Country by Country by Atinuke (Walker Books, 2019)

Africa Is My Home: A Child of the Amistad by Monica Edinger (Candlewick, 2015)

Africa Is Not a Country by Margy Burns Knight (First Avenue Editions, 2002)

Alejandria Fights Back!/¡La Lucha de Alejandria! by Leticia Hernández-Linares (The Femininist Press at CUNY, 2021)

All Are Welcome by Alexandra Penfold (Knopf Books for Young Readers, 2018)

Alma and How She Got Her Name by Juana Martinez-Neal (Candlewick, 2018)

The Ancient Maya by Jackie Maloy (Children's Press/Scholastic, 2010)

Areli is a Dreamer: The True Story by Areli Morales, a DACA Recipient by Areli Morales (Random House Studio, 2021)

Baby Goes to Market by Atinuke (Candlewick, 2019)

Bintou's Braids by Sylviane Diouf (Chronicle Books, 2004)

Bippity Bop Barbershop by Natasha Anastasia Tarpley (Little, Brown Books for Young Readers, 2009)

The Boy Who Harnessed the Wind by William Kamkwamba (Puffin Books, 2016)

A Brief Overview of the Aztec Empire (Baby Professor, 2020)

The Broken Spears by Miguel Leon-Portilla (Beacon Press, 2006)

Brown Boy by Daphnie Glenn (Palmetto Publishing, 2017)

Carmela, Full of Wishes by Matt De La Peña (G.P. Putnam's Sons Books for Young Readers 2018)

Carter Reads the Newspaper by Deborah Hopkinson (Peachtree Publishing, 2019)

Circle Unbroken by Margot Theis Raven (Square Fish, 2007)

Come On, Rain! by Karen Hesse (Scholastic, 1999)

Crown: An Ode to the Fresh Cut by Derrick Barnes (Agate Bolden, 2017)

Danza! By Duncan Tonatiuh (Abrams Books for Young Readers, 2017)

Dave the Potter: Artist, Poet, Slave by Laban Carrick Hill (Little, Brown Books for Young Readers, 2010)

The Day You Begin by Jacqueline Woodson (Nancy Paulsen Books, 2018)

Desmond and the Very Mean Word by Desmond Tutu (Candlewick, 2012)

A Different Pond by Bao Phi (Capstone Young Readers, 2017)

Dream Builder: The Story of Architect Philip Freelon by Kelly Starling Lyons (Lee & Low Books, 2020)

Dreamers by Yuyi Morales (Neal Porter Books, 2018)

Each Kindness by Jacqueline Woodson (Nancy Paulsen Books, 2012)

Emi's Curly, Coily, Cotton Candy Hair by Tina Olajide (CreateSpace, 2014)

The Farm in Spring by Jenny Giles (RIGBY, 2004)

Flossie and the Fox by Patricia C. McKissack (Dial Books, 1986)

Follow Me Down to Nicodemus Town by A. LaFaye (Albert Whitman, 2019)

For You Are a Kenyan Child by Kelly Cunnane (Atheneum Books for Young Readers, 2006)

Freedom Soup by Tami Charles (Candlewick, 2021)

Frida by Jonah Winter (Scholastic, 2002)

Furqan's First Flat Top/El Primer Corte de Mesita de Furqan by Robert Liu-Trujillo (Come Bien Books, 2016)

Galimoto by Karen Lynn Williams (HarperCollins, 1991)

Game by Walter Dean Myers (HarperTeen, 2009)

Grandma Comes to Stay by Ifeoma Onyefulu (Frances Lincoln Children's Books, 2015)

Grandpa, Is Everything Black Bad? by Sandy Lynne Holman (Culture Co Op, 1998)

Hair Love by Matthew A. Cherry (Kokila, 2019)

Hair Story by NoNieqa Ramos (Carolrhoda Books, 2021)

Hairs/Pelitos by Sandra Cisneros (Dragonfly Books, 1997)

Haiti: The First Black Republic by Frantz Derenoncourt, Jr. (Thorobred Books, 2021)

Hands Around the Library: Protecting Egypt's Treasured Books by Karen Leggett Abouraya (Dial Books, 2012)

Harvesting Hope: The Story of Cesar Chavez by Kathleen Krull (HMH Books for Young Readers, 2003)

Henry's Freedom Box: A True Story from the Underground Railroad by Ellen Levine (Scholastic, 2007)

Hey, Black Child by Useni Eugene Perkins (LB Kids, 2019)

Honey Baby Sugar Child by Alice Faye Duncan (Simon & Schuster, 2005)

Honey, I Love by Eloise Greenfield (HarperCollins, 2016)

I Am Alfonso Jones by Tony Medina (Tu Books, 2017)

I Am Enough by Grace Byers (Balzer + Bray, 2018)

I Am Every Good Thing by Derrick Barnes (Nancy Paulsen Books, 2020)

I Am Farmer: Growing an Environmental Movement in Cameroon by Miranda Paul (Millbrook Press, 2019)

I Believe I Can by Grace Byers (Balzer + Bray, 2020)

I Love My Hair! by Natasha Anastasia Tarpley (Little, Brown Books for Young Readers, 2001)

In The Time of the Drums by Kim L. Siegelson (Lee & Low, 2016)

Jabari Jumps by Gaia Cornwall (Candlewick, 2020)

Jambo Means Hello: Swahili Alphabet Book by Muriel Feelings (Puffin Books, 1992)

Janjak & Freda Go to the Iron Market by Elizabeth Turnbull (Light Messages, 2013)

Jazz by Walter Dean Myers (Holiday House, 2008)

Just Ask! Be Different, Be Brave, Be You by Sonia Sotomayor (Philomel Books, 2019)

The King of Kindergarten by Derrick Barnes (Nancy Paulsen Books 2019)

Kings and Queens of West Africa by Sylviane A. Diouf (Franklin Watts, 2000)

La Frontera: El viaje con papa/The Border: My Journey With Papa by Alfredo Alva and Deborah Mills (Barefoot Books, 2018)

Last Stop on Market Street by Matt de la Peña (G.P. Putnam's Sons Books for Young Readers, 2015)

Light as a Feather: The 42 Laws of Ma'at for Children by Kajara Nia Yaa Nebthet (Ingrid Russell, 2020)

A Likkle Miss Lou by Nadia Hohn (OwlKids, 2019)

The Little Book of Little Activists by Penguin Young Readers (Viking Books for Young Readers, 2017)

Looking Like Me by Walter Dean Myers (Carolrhoda Books, 2009)

Love by Matt de la Peña (G.P. Putnam's Sons Books for Young Readers, 2018)

Love Twelve Miles Long by Glenda Armand (Lee & Low, 2015)

M Is for Melanin: A Celebration of the Black Child by Tiffany Rose (little lee books, 2021)

Mama Africa! How Miriam Makeba Spread Hope with Her Song by Kathryn Erskine (FSG, 2017)

Mansa Musa and the Empire of Mali by P. James Oliver (CreateSpace, 2013)

The Matatu by Eric Walters (Orca Book Publishers, 2016)

Mi Papi Has a Motorcycle by Isabel Quintero (Kokila, 2019)

Moja Means One: Swahili Counting Book by Muriel Feelings (Puffin Books, 1992)

Momma, Did You Hear the News? by Sanya Whittaker Gragg (3g Publishing, 2021)

A Moon for Moe and Mo by Jane Breskin Zalben (Charlesbridge, 2018)

Moses: When Harriet Tubman Led Her People to Freedom by Carole Boston Weatherford (Hyperion, 2006)

My Rows and Piles of Coins by Tololwa M. Mollel (Clarion Books, 2019)

My Two Border Towns by David Bowles (Kokila, 2021)

A Name Like Mine: A Rhyming Story About Diversity and Inclusion by S.C. Sandore (2020)

Nelson Mandela: Long Walk to Freedom by Nelson Mandela, Abridged by Chris Van Wyk (Pan MacMillan, 2014)

Nelson Mandela: No Easy Walk to Freedom by Barry Denenberg (Scholastic, 2014)

Never Caught: The Story of Ona Judge by Erica Armstrong Dunbar (Aladdin, 2020)

Olmec Civilization for Kids (Baby Professor, 2017)

Nina: A Story of Nina Simone by Traci N. Todd (G.P. Putnam's Sons Books, 2021)

One Plastic Bag: Isatou Ceesay and the Recycling Women of the Gambia by Miranda Paul (Millbrook Press, 2015)

One Word from Sophia by Jim Averbeck (Atheneum Books for Young Readers, 2015)

Ostrich and Lark by Marilyn Nelson (Boyd Mills Press, 2012)

Our Skin: A First Conversation About Race by Megan Madison and Jessica Ralli (Rise x Penguin Workshop, 2021)

Planting Stories: The Life of Librarian and Storyteller Pura Belpré by Anika Aldamuy Denise (HarperCollins, 2019)

The Revolution of Evelyn Serrano by Sonia Manzano (Scholastic, 2014)

S Is for South Africa by Beverley Naidoo (Frances Lincoln Children's Books, 2011)

The Sad Night: The Story of an Aztec Victory and a Spanish Loss by Sally Schofer Mathews (Clarion Books, 2001)

Schomburg: The Man Who Built a Library by Carole Boston Weatherford (Candlewick, 2019)

Seeds of Change: Planting a Path to Peace by Jen Cullerton Johnson (Lee & Low, 2010)

Separate Is Never Equal by Duncan Tonatiuh (Harry N. Abrams, 2014)

A Shelter in Our Car by Monica Gunning (Lee & Low Books, 2013)

Show Way by Jacqueline Woodson (Nancy Paulsen Books, 2005)

Side by Side: The Story of Dolores Huerta and Cesar Chavez by Monica Brown (HarperCollins, 2010)

Sit-In: How Four Friends Stood Up by Sitting Down by Andrea Davis Pinkney (Little, Brown Books for Young Readers, 2010)

The 1619 Project: Born on the Water by Nikole Hannah-Jones and Renée Watson (Kokila, 2021)

Sojourner Truth's Step-Stomp Stride by Andrea Davis Pinkney (Little, Brown Books for Young Readers, 2009)

Soldier for Equality: José de la Luz Sáenz and the Great War by Duncan Tonatiuh (Harry N. Abrams, 2020)

Someday Is Now by Olugbemisola Rhuday-Perkovich (Seagrass Press, 2018)

Sonia Sotomayor: A Judge Grows in the Bronx by Jonah Winter (Atheneum Books for Young Readers, 2009)

Southwest Sunrise by Nikki Grimes (Bloomsbury Children's Books, 2020)

Sundiata: Lion King of Mali by David Wisniewski (Clarion, 1992)

Tap-Tap by Karen Lynn Williams (Clarion Books, 1995)

That's Not Fair!/¡No es justo! by Carmen Tafolla and Sharyll Teneyuca (Wings Press, 2010)

Thirteen Ways of Looking at a Black Boy by Tony Medina (Penny Candy Books, 2019)

Those Shoes by Maribeth Boelts (Candlewick, 2009)

A Thousand White Butterflies by Jessica Betancourt-Perez and Karen Lynn Williams (Charlesbridge, 2021)

The Undefeated by Kwame Alexander (Versify, 2019)

Under the Same Sun by Sharon Robinson (Scholastic, 2014)

Walking Home to Rosie Lee by A. LaFaye (Cinco Puntos Press, 2011)

Wangari Maathai: The Woman Who Planted Millions of Trees by Franck Prévot (Charlesbridge, 2017)

We Are Water Protectors by Carole Lindstrom (Roaring Book Press, 2020)

We Rise, We Resist, We Raise Our Voices by Wade Hudson and Cheryl Willis Hudson (Yearling, 2019)

Where Are You From? by Yamile Saied Méndez (HarperCollins, 2019)

Why Mosquitos Buzz in People's Ears by Verna Aardema (Puffin/Dial, 2004)

Yes! We Are Latinos by Alma Flor Ada and F. Isabel Campoy (Charlesbridge, 2016)

The Youngest Marcher by Cynthia Levinson (Atheneum Books for Young Readers, 2017)

Your Name Is a Song by Jamilah Thompkins-Bigelow (The Innovation Press, 2020)

REFERENCES

Acosta, M. M., Foster, M., & Houchen, D. F. (2018). "Why seek the living among the dead?" African American pedagogical excellence. *Journal of Teacher Education, 69*(4), 341–353.

Ansary, T. (2007). Education at risk: Fallout from a flawed report. *Edutopia.* https://www.edutopia.org/landmark-education-report-nation-risk

Anzaldúa, G. (1987). *Borderlands/La frontera: The new mestiza.* Aunt Lute Books.

Ascenzi-Moreno, L. (2018). Translanguaging and responsive assessment adaptations: Emergent bilingual readers through the lens of possibility. *Language Arts, 95*(6), 355-369.

Baker-Bell, A. (2020). Dismantling anti-black linguistic racism in English language arts classrooms: Toward an antiracist black language pedagogy. *Theory Into Practice, 59*(1), 8–21.

Baker-Bell, A. (2020). *Linguistic justice: Black language, literacy, identity, and pedagogy.* Routledge.

Baker-Bell, A. (2020). "We been knowin": Toward an antiracist language & literacy education. *Journal of Language and Literacy Education, 16*(1), n1.

Bever, L. (2016, April 7). https://www.washingtonpost.com/news/education/wp/2016/04/07/she-landed-on-her-face-video-shows-texas-school-police-officer-body-slam12-year-old-girl/

Bishop, R. S. (1990, March). Windows and mirrors: Children's books and parallel cultures. In *California State University reading conference: 14th annual conference proceedings.*

Braden, E. (2019). Book clubs. In D. Stephens, J.C. Harste, & J. A. Clyde (Eds.), *Reading revealed: 50 expert teachers share what they do and why they do it.* Scholastic.

Braden, E. G., Gibson, V., & Taylor-Gillette, R. (2020). Everything Black is NOT bad! Families and teachers engaging in critical discussions around race. *Talking Points, 31*(2), 2–12.

Briceño, A., & Klein, A. F. (2019). A second lens on formative reading assessment with multilingual students. *The Reading Teacher, 72*(5), 611–621.

Bryan, N. (2020). Shaking the bad boys: Troubling the criminalization of Black boys' childhood play, hegemonic White masculinity and femininity, and the school playground-to-prison pipeline. *Race Ethnicity and Education, 23*(5), 673–692.

Christensen, L. (2009). *Teaching for joy and justice: Re-imagining the language arts classroom.* Rethinking Schools.

Clay, M. M. (1991). *Becoming literate: The construction of inner control.* Heinemann.

Council, T. (2021). The souls of [Black] teachers: A participatory action research approach engaging teachers with communities against anti-Black policies and practices. Dissertation, Georgia State University.

Crenshaw, K. (1989). Demarginalizing the intersection of race and sex: A black feminist critique of antidiscrimination doctrine, feminist theory and antiracist politics. *Chi. Legal,* 139.

Crenshaw, K. W. (2006). Framing affirmative action. *Michigan Law Review, First Impressions, 105,* 123–133.

Delpit, L. D. (2018). The silenced dialogue: Power and pedagogy in educating other people's children. In *Thinking about Schools* (pp. 157–175). Routledge.

Derman-Sparks, L., & Ramsey, P. G. (2006). *What if all the kids are White? Anti-bias multicultural education with young children and families.* Teachers College Press.

Douglass, F. (1859). African civilization society. *Brotz, ed., Negro social and political thought.*

Drake, S., Auletto, A., & Cowen, J. (2019). Grading teachers: Race and gender differences in low evaluation ratings and teacher employment outcomes. *American Educational Research Journal, 56*(5), 1800–1833.

DuFresne, S. (2018). *The history of institutional racism in U.S. public schools.* Garn Press.

Dumas, M. J., & Ross, K. M. (2016). "Be real Black for me": Imagining BlackCrit in education. *Urban Education, 51*(4), 415–442.

Duncan-Smith, N. (2022, February 18). Florida first grader handcuffed and arrested at school two years ago now suffers from PTSD and separation anxiety, family says. https://www.yahoo.com/video/florida-first-grader-handcuffed-arrested-133000626.html

Edwards, J. (2021, October 21). A Texas school ban from boys from wearing long hair. Now parents are suing. https://www.washingtonpost.com/nation/2021/10/21/texas-students-long-hair-lawsuit/

Espinosa, C., & Ascenzi-Moreno, L. (2021). *Rooted in strength: Growing multilingual readers and writers, K–5.* Scholastic.

Fought, C. (2003). *Chicano English in context.* Springer.

Fountas, I., & Pinnell, G. S. (2007). *The continuum of literacy learning.* Heinemann.

Freire, P. (1970). *Pedagogy of the oppressed.* Seabury.

Freire, P. (1972). Education: domestication or liberation? *Prospects, 2*(2), 173–181.

Gay, G. (2010). Acting on beliefs in teacher education for cultural diversity. *Journal of Teacher Education, 61*(1–2), 143–152.

Gay, G. (2018). *Culturally responsive teaching: Theory, research, and practice.* Teachers College Press.

Gilliam, W. S., Maupin, A. N., Reyes, C. R., Accavitti, M. R., & Shic, F. (2016). *Do early educators' implicit biases regarding sex and race relate to behavior expectations and recommendations of preschool expulsions and suspensions?* Yale University Child Study Center.

Goodman, K. (1978) Kidwatching. An alternative to testing. *National Elementary Principal, 57*(4), 41–45.

Graves, D. H. (1983). *Writing: Teachers and children at work.* Heinemann.

Green, L. J. (2002). *African American English: a linguistic introduction.* Cambridge University Press.

Griffith, J. (2019). Bidding on Black students? School's mock slave auctions lead to state probe. *Governing.* https://www.governing.com/archive/bidding-on-black-students-schools-mock-slave-auctions-lead-to-state-probe.html

Grissom, J. A., & Redding, C. (2016). Discretion and disproportionality: Explaining the underrepresentation of high-achieving students of color in gifted programs. AERA Open.

Hammond, B., Hoover, M. E. R., & McPhail, I. P. (2005). *Teaching African American learners to read: Perspectives and practices.* International Reading Association.

Hart, B., & Risley, T. R. (1992). American parenting of language-learning children: Persisting differences in family-child interactions observed in natural home environments. *Developmental Psychology, 28*(6), 1096.

Hobson, M. (2014). Color blind or color brave? [Video]. TED Conferences. https://www.ted.com/talks/mellody_hobson_color_blind_or_color_brave?language=en

hooks, b. (1999). *All about love: New visions.* Harper Perennial.

Howard, E. (2010). *To-morrow: A peaceful path to real reform.* Cambridge University Press.

Hurt, J. W. (2018). "Why are the gifted classes so White?" Making space for gifted Latino students. *Journal of Cases in Educational Leadership, 21*(4), 112–130.

Jackson, J. E., & Green, L. (2005) Tense and aspectual *be* in child African American English. In: H. J. Verkuyl, H. de Swart H., & A. van Hout (Eds.) *Perspectives on aspect: Studies in Theoretical Psycholinguistics,* vol 32. Springer, Dordrecht.

Johnson, L. L., Bryan, N., & Boutte, G. (2019). Show us the love: Revolutionary teaching in (un) critical times. *The Urban Review, 51*(1), 46–64.

Jones, K., & Okun, T. (2001). White supremacy culture. *Dismantling Racism: A Workbook for Social Change Groups.* ChangeWork.

Kendi, I. X. (2018). Black doctoral studies: The radically antiracist idea of Molefi Kete Asante. *Journal of Black Studies, 49*(6), 542–558.

Kendi, I. X. (2019). *How to be an antiracist.* One World.

King, J., & Swartz, E. (2018). *Heritage knowledge in the curriculum.* Routledge.

Ladson-Billings, G. (1998). Just what is critical race theory and what's it doing in a nice field like education? *International Journal of Qualitative Studies in Education, 11*(1), 7–24.

Lee-Heart, K. (2018). "Why Keisha can't write": The marginalization of Black student writing. *Learning for Justice.*

Lesesne, P. (2020). *A sistah circle of seven: Black women's self-perceptions of their Teach for America (TFA) experiences in the U.S. Mid-Atlantic region* [Unpublished doctoral dissertation]. University of Pennsylvania.

Love, B. L. (2019). *We want to do more than survive: Abolitionist teaching and the pursuit of educational freedom.* Beacon Press.

Lyon, G. E. (1999). *Where I'm from: Where poems are from.* Absey & Co.

MacDorman, M., Thoma, M., Declcerq, E., & Howell, E. (2021). Racial and ethnic disparities in maternal mortality in the United States using enhanced vital records, 2016-17. *American Journal of Public Health,* 111, no. 9: 1673–81.

Majors, Y. J. (2015). *Shoptalk: Lessons in teaching from an African American hair salon.* Teachers College Press.

Miller, E. T. (2015). Discourses of Whiteness and Blackness: An ethnographic study of three young children learning to be White. *Ethnography and Education,* 10(2), 137–153.

Mills, H. (2004). *Looking closely and listening carefully: Learning literacy through inquiry.* National Council of Teachers of English.

Moll, L., Amanti, C., Neff, D., & Gonzalez, N. (1992). Funds of knowledge for teaching: Using a qualitative approach to connect homes and classrooms. *Theory into Practice,* 31(2),132–141.

Morris, M. (2016). *Pushout: The criminalization of Black girls in schools.* The New Press.

Muhammad, G. (2020). Cultivating genius: *An equity framework for culturally and historically responsive literacy.* Scholastic.

Muller, M. (2020). Pre-service teachers engage young children in equity work. *Journal of Early Childhood Teacher Education,* 1-16.

Myers, M. (2019). Browse bags. In D. Stephens, J. C. Harste, and J. A. Clyde (Eds.), *Reading instruction: What, why and how.* Scholastic.

National Council of Teachers of English (2015). Resolution on the Need for Diverse Children's and Young Adult Books. Retrieved from: https://ncte.org/statement/diverse-books/

National Council of Teachers of English (2017). Statement on Classroom Libraries. Retrieved from: https://ncte.org/statement/classroom-libraries/

No Child Left Behind (NCLB) Act of 2001, Pub. L. No. 107-110,115, Stat. 1425 (2002).

Noe-Bustamante, L., Mora, L., & Lopez, M. H. (2020). Latinx used by just 3% of U.S. Hispanics. *Pew Research Center's Hispanic Trends Project.* Retrieved from https://www.pewresearch.org/hispanic/wp-content/uploads/sites/5/2020/08/PHGMD_2020.08.11_Latinx_FINAL.pdf

Ntiri, D. W. (2009). Toward a functional and culturally salient definition of literacy. *Adult Basic Education and Literacy Journal,* 3(2), 97–104.

O'Connor, C., Hill, L. D., & Robinson, S. R. (2009). Who's at risk in school and what's race got to do with it? *Review of Research in Education,* 33, 1–34. http://www.jstor.org/stable/40588116

O'Rourke, B. (2018). Bringing a dying language back to life. *The Harvard Gazette.* A-dying-language-comes-to-life-in-classroom

Okonofua, J. A., Walton, G. M., & Eberhardt, J. L. (2016). A vicious cycle: A social–psychological account of extreme racial disparities in school discipline. *Perspectives on Psychological Science,* 11(3), 381–398.

Okun, B. F. (1998). *Understanding diverse families: What practitioners need to know.* Guilford Press.

Paley, V. G. (2000). *White teacher: With a new preface.* Harvard University Press.

Pérez Huber, L., & Solorzano, D. G. (2015). Racial microaggressions as a tool for critical race research. *Race Ethnicity and Education,* 18(3), 297–320.

Perry, T., & Delpit, L. D. (Eds.). (1998). *The real Ebonics debate: Power, language, and the education of African-American children.* Beacon Press.

Perry, T., Steele, C. M., & Hilliard III, A. G. (2004). *Young, gifted, and black: Promoting high achievement among African-American students.* Beacon Press.

Plutchik, R. (2001). The nature of emotions: Human emotions have deep evolutionary roots, a fact that may explain their complexity and provide tools for clinical practice. *American Scientist,* 89(4), 344–350.

Rafa, A., Erwin, B., Brixley, E., McCann, M., & Perez, Z. (2020). *50 state comparisons: English learner policy.* Education Commission of the United States.

Rasinski, T. V. (2006). Reading fluency instruction: Moving beyond accuracy, automaticity, and prosody. *The Reading Teacher,* 59: 704–706.

Ray, K. W. (1999). *Wondrous Words: writers and writing in the elementary classroom.* National Council of Teachers of English.

Redd, T. M., & Schuster Webb, K. (2005). *A teacher's introduction to African American English: What a writing teacher should know.* National Council of Teachers of English.

Reid, T. R. (2005). Spanish at school translates to suspension. *Washington Post.* https://www.washingtonpost.com/archive/politics/2005/12/09/spanish-at-school-translates-to-suspension/8df9e017-f704-4a2b-af67-485d10316794/

Rickford, J. (1996). *What is Ebonics?* Linguistic Society of America.

Rodriguez, S. C. (2017). Becoming a writer: Emergent bilinguals use of language resources in an English only kindergarten writing workshop. *Perspectives and Provocations,* 6(1), 37.

Rosales, J., & Walker, T. (2018). The racist beginnings of standardized testing. *National Education Association,* 73(2), 88–96.

Russell, J. R., & Rickford, R. J. (2000). *Spoken soul: The story of Black English.* John Wiley & Sons.

Salaam, K. Y. (1979). Women's rights are human rights! *The Black Scholar,* 10(6–7), 9–14.

Salaam, K. Y. (1978). *Revolutionary love: Poems and essays.* Ahidiana-Habari.

Serravallo, J. (2019). *A teacher's guide to reading conferences: Grades K–8.* Heinemann.

Smitherman, G., & McGinnis, J. (1977). Black language and Black liberation. *Black Books Bulletin.*

Smitherman, G. (2006). *Word from the mother: Language and African Americans.* Routledge.

Solórzano, D. G. (1998). Critical race theory, race and gender microaggressions, and the experience of Chicana and Chicano scholars. *International Journal of Qualitative Studies in Education,* 11(1), 121–136.

Sperry, D. E., Sperry, L. L., & Miller, P. J. (2019). Reexamining the verbal environments of children from different socioeconomic backgrounds. *Child Development,* 90(4), 1303–1318.

Strickland, D. (1998). *Teaching phonics today: A primer for educators.* International Literacy Association.

Tatum, B. L. (2017). *Crime, violence and minority youths.* Routledge.

Thornton, N.A. (2017). Culturally relevant literacy instruction: Promoting shifts in teachers' beliefs and practices. In C. Martin & D. Polly (Eds.), *Handbook of research on teacher education and professional development,* (pp. 310–338). IG! Global.

Turner, B. S. (1990). Outline of a theory of citizenship. *Sociology,* 24(2), 189–217.

U.S. Department of Education. (2016). Office of Special Education and Rehabilitative Services. In *38th Annual Report to Congress on the Implementation of the Individuals with Disabilities Education Act, 2016.*

Valenzuela Jr, A. (1999). Gender roles and settlement activities among children and their immigrant families. *American Behavioral Scientist,* 42(4), 720-742.

Walker, V. S. (1996). *Their highest potential: An African American school community in the segregated South.* University of North Carolina Press.

Watson, D., Hagopian, J., & Au, W. (Eds.). (2018). *Teaching for Black lives.* Rethinking Schools.

Weldon, T. L. (2000). Reflections on the Ebonics controversy. *American Speech,* 75(3), 275–277.

Wheeler, R. S., & Swords, R. (2006). *Code-switching: Teaching standard English in urban classrooms.* National Council of Teachers.

Wiggins, L., Durkin, M., Esler, A., Lee, L., Zahorodny, W., Rice, C., Yeargin-Allsopp, M., Dowling, N., Hall-Lande, J., Morrier, M., Christensen, D., Shenouda, J., & Baio, J. (2019). Disparities in documented diagnoses of Autism Spectrum Disorder based on demographic, individual, and service factors. *Autism Research,* 13, (3), pp. 464–473.

Wynter-Hoyte, K., Long, S., Frazier, J., & Jackson, J. (2021). Liberatory praxis in preservice teacher education: claiming Afrocentricity as foundational in critical language and literacy teaching. *International Journal of Qualitative Studies in Education,* 1–22.

Yusem, D. (2018). Youth Engagement in restorative justice. In M. Thorsborne, N. Riestenberg, & G. McCluskey (Eds.) *Getting more out of restorative practice in schools: Practical approaches to improve school wellbeing and strengthen community engagement.* Jessica Kingsley Publishers.

INDEX

A

"achievement gap" (dog-whistle term), 44, 45–46
activism, books on, 134–135
acts and laws, discriminatory, 36–39, 48
adjusting (strategy), 136
affirming students' language use, 108–110
African American Language (AAL), 33, 113–123
  and comprehension, 150
  Kamania's use of, 107
  in reading conferences, 111–112
  and translanguaging (instructional unit), 122
  unpacking (self-examination activity), 116
African cultures and languages (instructional unit), 118–119
African Diaspora, history and languages of (instructional unit), 120–121
African Ma'at principles, 79–80
African peoples' pre-enslavement contributions (instructional unit), 62–63
analyzing (strategy), 136
anchor charts, 140, 143, 160, 169, 183
Angelou, Maya, 12–13
assessments, 41–43, 179–182
assimilation, as purpose of schooling, 36, 54–55
"at-risk readers" (dog-whistle term), 44, 47–48
authentic texts, 147
authentic writing, as purposeful, 158
authenticity, in classroom community, 90–91

B

Baldwin, James, 154
behavior management, commonly biased, 40–43
  with African Ma'at principles, 79–80
beliefs about writing (self-examination activity), 163
Belpré, Pura, 17, 175
Bethune, Mary McLeod, 17
biases, in school practices, 40–43
  "big topic," vs. detailed writing, 176
biases, prevalence of, 32–34
bilingual education movement, 16
bilingualism, Sanjuana's, 59
Binet, Alfred, 45
biography, 174–175
BIPOC representation in children's literature, 60–61, 67
Bishop, Rudine Sims, 51, 52, 67, 134, 146, 156
Black Codes during Reconstruction, 36
Black Lives Matter movement, 16
book clubs, 153–154

family (engagement), 104
book discussion, to fuel introspection, 33
books, by title
  that build community, 81–82
  as mentor texts by topic, 170–175
  for instructional units, 117–122, 127–128
  for interactive read-alouds, 134–135
  on social injustice, 155–156
Boutte, Gloria, 10–11, 18
Brigham, Carl, 45
browse bags, 145–146, 150

C

call-and-response, in African American Language (AAL), 115, 122
Carmela, Full of Wishes (Matt De la Peña), 143–144, 172
Carolinas, enslaved peoples' contributions to, 62–63
celebrations, writing, 74, 183–184
characters in children's literature, demographics of main, 60–61
Chicano English, 124
children's literature, 52
  demographics of main characters, 60–61
  guidelines for selecting, 64–65
  as windows, mirrors, sliding glass doors, 52
class activities
  auditing classroom library, 67–70
  co-creating classroom norms, 77–78
classism, books on, 135
classroom community, building authenticity in, 90–91
classroom environments, supportive, 130
classroom library, 51, 145
  examining, 65–70
classroom norms, culturally inclusive, 73–78
classroom practices, bias in, 40–43
"code-switching," 111
colonialism, literacy and, 53, 79, 128
"colorblind" approach, 19, 39–41
"colorbrave" approach, 41
communication with families, modes of, 98
communities, engaging with, 93–104
community of writers, creating, 163–165
community-building activities, 83–91
  books for, 81–82
conference form, for writer's workshop, 177
conferring, 158, 176–177
  planning guide for, 185
connections, text-to-self, -text, -world, 144
consonants, final, in Mexican American Language (MxAL), 125
Conant, James Bryant, 45
Cooper, Anna J., 17

Cooperative Children's Book Center (CCBC), 60–61, 67
Coppin, Fanny Jackson, 17
Crenshaw, Kimberlé, 31
criminalization of Black boys' play, 40
critiquing (strategy), 136
Crown: An Ode to the Fresh Cut (Derrick Barnes), 111–112, 167
cueing systems, 147, 151
cultural identity, dimensions of, 25–29
curricula, examining, 60–65, 100

D

deficit-oriented beliefs, 37–38, 94, 97
  disrupting, as principle of revolutionary love, 19–22
Delpit, Lisa, 18, 33
developmental reading stages, literacy timeline through, 58–59
dialogue, 177
digital literacy, 21, 58
dimensions of identity, 25–31
discomfort, being comfortable with, 76
diversity in children's literature, 60–62, 64–70
"dog-whistle terms," 44–49
Douglass, Frederick, 10, 53
dress code, investigating for bias, 41–43

E

Each Kindness (Jacqueline Woodson), 79, 81, 139–140
economics instructional unit, culturally inclusive, 98
Edgar cut, 40
educational policies, racist, history of, 36–38
Educational Testing Service (ETS), 45
Emanuel Nine, 38
emotion wheel (chart), 91
engagements, family, 101–104
English-only instruction, 36, 37, 41–43, 54–56
enslavement, literacy and, 53, 89, 120
Escalante, Jaime, 17
Eurocentricity in curricula, 13, 45, 60–62
"evidence-based" initiatives, 37

F

families, engaging with, 93–104
Family Read-Alouds, 103
"Family Time," for building authenticity, 90
feelings, characters', determining, 143–144
Fountas and Pinnell, 135
Freire, Paulo, 13, 21, 48, 131

G

Gay, Geneva, 18, 101
Gibson, Valente', 8, 90, 104, 111–112, 116, 120–121, 153–154, 167

gifted education programs, 40–43
"Gullah," 113

H

habitual *be*, in African American Language
    (AAL), 114, 115, 122–123
"Hair Moments" (instructional unit), 158,
    165–168, 176
    mentor texts for, 170–171
hair styles, 36, 40, 41, 81, 86, 176
    Eliza's, 64
Hey, Black Child (Useni Eugene Perkins), in
    interactive read-aloud, 135, 137–138
high-needs, as normalizing Whiteness, 44
Hilliard, Asa, 22
Hobson, Melody, 41
home languages, honoring, 15, 106–112,
    115–116, 128, 130, 131, 151, 179
home literacy practices, 53, 57–59, 79, 92,
    97–101, 133
"Honey, I Love" (Eloise Greenfield), 88
"Honey, I Love" poems (community-building
    activity), 88–89
hooks, bell, 13, 18–19
human right, literacy as, 51

I

I see..., I think..., and *I wonder...* chart,
    example of, 63
Idar, Jovita, 17
identity web (self-examination activity),
    25–26
identities
    authors', 14–17, 27
    students', honored in community-
        building activities, 83–91
immigration, books on, 135
independent reading, 111, 130, 141, 144,
    145–146
independent writing, 158, 165, 176, 185
Indian Boarding Schools, 35, 37
Indian Welfare Act, 37
individualism in classroom, 74
inferring (strategy), 136
injustice, texts related to, 153–156
instructional units, culturally inclusive, 98,
        116–123, 127–128, 158, 165–168, 176
    on African American Language and
        translanguaging, 122
    on African cultures and languages,
        118–119
    on African Diaspora, history and
        languages of, 120–121
    economics, culturally inclusive, 98
    on geography relative to Africa, 117
    "Hair Moments," 158, 165–168, 176
    on kindness, 139–140, 180–182
    about Mexico's history, cultures, and
        language, 127–128
intergenerational writing (engagement),
    102
Irvine, Jacqueline Jordan, 18
"-isms," 32–34

J

Jackson, Helen Hunt, 22

K

Kaepernick, Colin, 154
Kendi, Ibram X., 39
kidwatching, 147–151, 176
kindness, units on, 139–140, 180–182
King, Joyce, 97
King Jr., Martin Luther, 21, 22
knowing students, as principle of
    revolutionary love, 19–22

L

Ladson-Billings, Gloria, 18, 33, 38
language beliefs, exploring (self-
    examination activity), 108–110
language use, students', responses to,
    108–110
Latine, 14
Latine in KidLit, 66
"learning to read" vs. "reading to learn," 48
level the playing field, as normalizing
    Whiteness, 37, 44
Lewis, John, 22
linguistic expectations, investigating for
    bias, 41–43
linguistic repertoire, drawn on, 111, 126,
    179
literacy, 51–52
    non-traditional loci of, 52, 59, 99–101,
        146
    political history of, 53–56
    suppressed during enslavement, 53, 89
    timeline, creating (self-examination
        activity), 57–59
literacy skills, practiced in interactive read-
    loud, 138
literary societies, Black, 53
love, as principle of revolutionary love,
    19–22
    courageous, 13
    "thin" vs. revolutionary, 10
Lyiscott, Jamila, 116
Lyon, George Ella, 83, 103

M

mainstream English (ME), 56, 66, 106–110,
        161
    books in, 65
    Kamania's use of, 107
    translanguaging with, 111–115, 123,
        124–128
maintaining fluency (strategy), 136
making connections (strategy), 136
maternal outcomes, among Black vs. White
    women, 31
McDonald, Caitlyn, 8, 60, 61, 78, 79–80, 116
meaning-making processes, 147
meetings and conferences, 100
mental movie, 168
mentor texts, 134–135, 158, 170–175
    not reflecting Black and Latine students,
        64
    planning guide for, 185
Mexican American children, 36–37
    Sanjuana as example of, 54–55

Mexican American Language (MxAL),
        124–125
    and translanguaging (instructional unit),
        128
Mexico's history, cultures, and language
    (instructional units), 127–128
microaggressions
    anti-Latine, 126–127
    recognizing Eliza's own, 94
    toward families, 95–96
mini-lessons, 141–144, 158
    planning guide for, 185
    in writer's workshop, 167–169
miscue analysis, 147, 151
mock auction, 40
Moll, Luis, 18
Morales, Yuyi, 165
morphology
    in African American Language (AAL), 114
    in Mexican American Language (MxAL),
        125
Morrison, Toni, 10

N

name stories, 101, 171–172
narrative writing, 172–173
National Commission on Excellence in
    Education, 47
National Council of Teachers of English
    (NCTE), 66
National Research Council, 48
Native American Boarding Schools, 35, 37
Native American children, 35–37
Naturalization Act of 1790, 38–39
needs-based teaching of reading, 152–153
No Child Left Behind (NCLB), 37, 48
norms, co-creating with students
    (classroom activity), 77–78
norms in school, traditional, culturally
    inclusive alternatives to, 74–76
note-taking, 147–151

O

oppression vs. agency, in dimension of
    social identity, 28–29
oral history (community-building activity),
    89
oral storytelling, 59
    in writer's workshop, 165–167
"Our Stories" chart, 164–165
over-correcting students' language use,
    108–110, 150
#OwnVoices authors, 65, 66, 68

P

Pantoja, Antonia, 17
parent-teacher conferences, 100
perfectionism, 74
"-phobias," 32–34
phonics, 147
phonology
    in African American Language (AAL), 114
    in Mexican American Language (MxAL),
        125
plural marker (*s*), dropped in Mexican
    American Language (MxAL), 125

police brutality, in texts, 155–156
policies, racist, 38–41
politics in teaching, 38–41
Positive Behavior Interventions and Supports (PBIS), 37
possessives, in African American Language (AAL), 115
power hoarding, 74
practices with families, culturally inclusive, 99–104
pragmatics, in African American Language (AAL), 114
prayers, 59, 146
predicting (strategy), 136
pre-reading, 135
pronunciation, influenced by African American Language (AAL), 150, 152–153
punctuation, 177
punishment vs. reward, inequity of, 78

Q
quick-writes, 168

R
Race to the Top (RTT), 37
RAFT, 159
"Raised by" poems (community-building activity), 86–87
Rankin, Jeremiah, 22
read-alouds
    family (engagement), 103
    in instructional units on AAL, 117–122
    in instructional units on MxAL, 127–128
    interactive, 134–140
reader's workshop, 129–155
reading assessment, 146–151
reading conferences, one-to-one, 145
reading interest inventories, 132–133
reading processes, mini-lessons on, 141–144
reading the world (Freire), 48, 131
"reading to learn," 48
resources
    about African American Language (AAL), 113
    for building diverse classroom library, 66
    about culturally inclusive norms, 77
    about Mexican American Language (MxAL), 125
Response to Intervention (RTI), 37
responses to students' language use, 108–110
restorative justice practices, 91
Revolutionary Love, 13, 19–22
    in action (authors' stories), 27, 79–80, 90, 94, 107
    need for (authors'stories), 33, 54–55, 64, 126
rubrics, holistic, for writing assessment, 180–182

S
Salaam, Kalamu ya, 13, 17
Scholastic Aptitude Test (SAT), 45
school practices/policies, investigating for bias (self-examination activity), 40–43
schooling, purposes of, 35–38

"scientifically based research" (dog-whistle term), 44, 46–47
searching for and using information (strategy), 136
segregation in schooling, 35–38
selecting books for read-alouds, 134–135
self-correction, 150, 152–153
self-examination activities, 24
    African American Language (AAL), unpacking, 116
    identity web, building, 25–26
    language, beliefs about, exploring, 108–110
    literacy timelines, creating 57–59
    microaggressions, mining, 95
    microaggressions, rebutting 127
    school practices/policies for bias, investigating, 41–43
    strengths in writing ,noticing, 179
    social identity and stereotypes, 30–31
    social identity, labeling dimensions of, 28–29
    writing and writers, beliefs about, examining, 163
    writing practices, reflecting on, 161
self-examination, critical, for biases, 32–34
sensory details anchor chart, 169
"separate but equal" education, 36
share time, 158, 185
sharing written work, 178
sink-or-swim method of instruction, 55
"Six Room Poem" (Georgia Heard), 169
"small moments," 165, 168
small-group instruction, 151–154
Smith, Mukarramah, 8
    teaching African Ma'at principles, 79–80
social identity
    labeling dimensions of (self-examination activity), 28–29
    and stereotypes (self-examination activity), 30–31
Social Justice Books, 66
socializing children, as purpose of education, 35–38
solving words (strategy), 136
Sotomayor, Sonia, 82, 175
"Spanglish," 124
Spanish, books in, 65, 171
"speaking correctly," 113–114
special education, investigating for bias, 40–43
standardized tests, 45–46
stereotypes, 30–31
storytelling, 75
    as literacy practice, 50–51
    in writer's workshop, 165–167
strategic actions, 12 systems of, 136
    instruction, 176
strengths in writing, noticing (self-examination activity), 179
stress patterns, of Mexican American Language (MxAL), 125
students as readers, 131–133
students as writers, 161–162

students' identities, honored in community-building activities, 83–91
students' racial identities, books on, 135
Suber, Sara, 8, 139–140, 147
summarizing (strategy), 136
Swartz, Ellen, 97
syntax, in African American Language (AAL), 114
synthesizing (strategy), 136

T
talking, 75
talking circles, 91
tests, standardized, 45–46
text sets, class and family (engagement), 104
thinking deeply about text, 142–143
"third-grade indicator" (dog-whistle term), 48–49
translanguaging, 111–112
transparency with mistakes, teacher, 74
Tubman, Harriet, 10
Tyson, James, 22

V
Valenzuela, Angela, 18
vocabulary, unfamiliar, 135

W
We Need Diverse Books, 66
West African and African Diaspora languages, 114–115
"Where I'm From" memoirs (engagement), 103
"Where I'm From" poems (community-building activity), 83–85, 143
White people who fought for equity, 22
Whiteness as norm
    in curriculum, 18–19, 44, 49, 100
    microaggressions and, 20, 38, 95–96
whole-part-whole method, 147
windows, mirrors, and sliding glass doors, 52
    in classroom libraries, 65–70
    in classroom library, 51–52, 65, 67, 134, 146, 156, 185
Witherspoon, Jacqui, 8
Woodson, Jacqueline, as model, 163, 165
writer's workshop, 157–186
    conference form, 177
    interest survey, 162
    planning guide for, 185
writing and writers, beliefs about (self-examination activity), 163
writing assessment, 179–182
writing celebrations, 183–184
written word, worship of, 75

Y
YouTube videos, 45, 116, 117, 118, 120, 122, 127